Praise for Gu*tteridge and McKay*

"McKay and Gutteridge have created a unique and humorous novel about the search for Mr. Right in which God plays matchmaker. Jessie's dialogue with God is just like one between friends. She laughs, argues and talks about her hopes and dreams. This is a great novel to kick back and escape reality with."
— Romantic Times Review: 4 ½ stars on *Never the Bride*

"The plot is ingenious. The writing is clever and funny (a little bit like *Bridget Jones Diary*). The romance is, well, romantic. But what makes this novel special is that we get a glimpse of God..."
— Leigh DeVore, Charismamag.com on *Never the Bride*

"A great story, this book will have you laughing until the end."
— Crosswayz Reviews on *Never the Bride*

"In *Never the Bride* Cheryl McKay and Rene Gutteridge have crafted a well-written, sometimes funny, sometimes bittersweet story. The characters are fully fleshed out; Jessie is controlling, but loveable, dreaming up romances with nearly every man she meets. It's a challenge to portray the Almighty as a character and the authors have done a marvelous job. The description and the dialogue are quite creative and often laugh-out-loud funny. The message of the story is one that everyone – married or single – can take to heart."
— Paula K. Parker, Buddyhollywood.com

"The script is tight and often compelling, the dialogue sparks and the production values are first-rate. A nice change-of-pace from the kind of hip cynicism that seems to infuse even the most genial of Hollywood family films these days."
— Seattle Post-Intelligencer on *The Ultimate Gift*

"With so many lessons to be taught and learned (add the subjects of family, dreams, love, gratitude and others to the list above), the movie bites off more than it should be able to chew. Yet Cheryl McKay's screenplay, adapted from a novel by motivational speaker Jim Stovall, hums forward engagingly without feeling rushed or overstuffed."
— FDL Reporter on *The Ultimate Gift*

"Screenplay writer Cheryl McKay does a nice job avoiding corny dialogue and keeping conversations natural and believable without resorting to the usual Hollywood shortcut of using profanity to convey intensity."
— Carolyn Arends / Christianity Today on *The Ultimate Gift*

"No Christian fiction novelist can tickle a funny bone like Gutteridge, and her third installment in the Occupational Hazards series (*Scoop*; *Snitch*) doesn't disappoint... Gutteridge is a pro, from smooth point of view changes to snappy dialogue. What could have been clichéd slapstick turns into unbridled hilarity in her capable hands, and the laughter doesn't stop until the wheels touch the tarmac."
— From Publishers Weekly on *Skid*

"Gutteridge is an adept and talented writer with a good sense of humor."
— Publishers Weekly

NOVELIZATIONS:
How to Adapt Scripts Into Novels

A Writing Guide for
Screenwriters and Authors

By Rene Gutteridge

Boo Series (Boo, Boo Who, Boo Hiss, Boo Humbug)
Escapement
Ghost Writer
Greetings from the Flipside (with Cheryl McKay)
Heart of the Country
Listen
Misery Loves Company
My Life as a Doormat
Never the Bride (with Cheryl McKay)
Possession
The Storm Series (Splitting Storm, Storm Gathering, Storm Surge)
The Occupational Hazards Series (Scoop, Snitch, Skid)
Troubled Waters
The Ultimate Gift novelization

Coming Soon
Just 18 Summers (with Michelle Cox, Marshal Younger & Torry Martin)
Old Fashioned (with Rik Swartzwelder)

By Cheryl McKay

Never the Bride (screenplay)
Never the Bride a novel (with Rene Gutteridge)
Finally the Bride: Finding Hope While Waiting
Finally Fearless: Journey from Panic to Peace
The Ultimate Gift (screenplay)
The Ultimate Life (screen story)
A Friend for Maddie (screenplay)
Gigi: God's Little Princess DVD (screenplay)
Wild & Wacky, Totally True Bible Stories Series (with Frank Peretti)
Spirit of Springhill: Miners, Wives, Widows, Rescuers, & Their Children Tell True Stories of Springhill's Coal Mining Disasters

Coming Soon
Song of Springhill: a love story

NOVELIZATIONS: HOW TO ADAPT SCRIPTS INTO NOVELS
A Writing Guide for Screenwriters and Authors

Cover Design by Christopher Price

Excerpts from "Greetings from the Flipside" by Rene Gutteridge &
Cheryl McKay, used by permission of B&H Publishing, TN.

Excerpts from the screenplay "Greetings from the Flipside" by Cheryl
McKay, used by permission.

Excerpts from "Old Fashioned" the novel by Rene Gutteridge and Rik
Swartzwelder, used by permission of Tyndale House Publishers, IL.

Excerpts from the screenplay "Old Fashioned" by Rik Swartzwelder,
used by permission.

Excerpts from "Heart of the Country" the novel by Rene Gutteridge
and John Ward, used by permission of Tyndale House Publishers, IL.

Excerpts from the screenplay "Heart of the Country" by John Ward,
used by permission.

ISBN-13: 9780615962153
ISBN-10: 0615962157

Published in the United States of America
Copyright © 2014 by Rene Gutteridge, Inc. & Cheryl McKay
2014—First Edition

TABLE OF CONTENTS

Chapter One

OVERVIEW

Cheryl McKay (aka The Screenwriter)

What is a Novelization?

There is a new trend percolating in the writing industry with *novelizations*. I'm not talking about serials that show up on bookshelves to match every episode of your favorite TV crime drama or the book spin-offs depicting your child's favorite TV or movie characters. Rather, there is a different trend that began in the endlessly imaginative world of Hollywood around 2008.

Most writers are familiar with the custom of taking a book and adapting it for the silver screen. That's been around since *Oliver Twist, Ben Hur,* and *Rip Van Winkle's* clever arrivals. But what is this reversal? Can we take screenplays — even before they are filmed — and turn them into novels? Can these novels have a life of their own, independent of a film or television release?

The novelization process, as its own piece of artistry, is a whole different form of writing; it's literally the opposite of book-to-screen adaptations and it's gaining popularity. This topic that — just a few years ago, you'd never heard of — is suddenly on the roster of classes at screenwriting, film, and fiction writing conferences. Rene and I have even had the chance to teach some of those.

We find this new trend exciting. Perhaps it's because we had the privilege of getting involved on the front end of its newfound popularity before *we* had even heard of it.

Our Story

Our journey began in 2007. We met after Rene wrote the novelized version of my screenplay for *The Ultimate Gift* after it had been made into a feature film. What was unusual about that was the screenplay was already based on a book, penned by Jim Stovall. However, the producers and the publisher thought there would be value in releasing a second novel that closely matched the feature film. Rather than just rereleasing the original novel with the movie poster on the front, Thomas Nelson Publishers hired Rene to novelize my screenplay and then they published it in time for the feature film's release.

This creative process gave us a fresh idea. What if we could get publishers to commission novels based on screenplays, even if those screenplays hadn't yet been made into films?

If you are a screenwriter, can you imagine not having to wait for your movie to get cast, filmed, posted, and distributed to the nearest theater or Redbox to find an audience? Wouldn't you love to start building an audience sooner?

Now you can, with what we are going to teach you through this book.

When Rene read my script *Never the Bride*, she knew she wanted my quirky rom-com to be the first story we worked on together. Our dream came true! In early 2008, when this new trend was barely even a concept, Random House contracted us for the novelization of *Never the Bride*.

Thus began the journey that has continued since that day. Collectively, we have seven of these in publication or soon-to-be-released, and we plan to do more. We have learned so much about the script-to-novel writing process. We now want to share that with you. It is a different art form altogether from adapting books into scripts or writing novels from scratch.

Why Novelizations?

You may be wondering what the motive is for a

screenwriter or a novelist to get involved in this process. For those writers who can do both forms of writing — why would you want to pen two projects based on the same material?

Well, it's simple. The film industry is risk-adverse. Check out the slate of films releasing on any given Friday. You will notice most of these projects are based on something preexisting: a novel, a nonfiction book, a comic book, a character, a true story, a historical event, a sequel, prequel or spin-off of a prior film or TV series, a remake of a prior film. (Did you know *Les Miserables* has been adapted into film over ten times?) Hollywood loves to know they have a built-in audience with whom to start. Otherwise, they are too afraid no one will shell out the big bucks to fill their stadium-style theater seats.

Yet screenwriters have good ideas for stories too, right? New, fresh, original. Naturally, not all screenwriters are novelists, just like most novelists wouldn't know how to adapt their books into screenplays. (The writing rules couldn't be more opposite!) In recent years, if executives came across a project they liked but they wanted to see if there was an audience for it, they might suggest the screenwriter get their project novelized and published first.

Besides having your story published, the benefit for the screenwriter is to be able to take meetings with studios, TV networks, and producers, and talk about how her story sold first as a novel. This gives the impression that someone else considered that story worth buying. It will give that screenwriter a leg up on other scripts in the slush pile that have no track record.

There have also been success stories in the independent publishing realm if a screenwriter released a novelization on her own and it gained a big audience. Studio executives pay attention to ebook sales, whether books are traditionally published or not, especially if there's a large following made obvious by chatty readers in book forums. (According to an executive at a conference speaking on novelizations, it may only take the sale of 10,000 copies of an independently published novel to capture the eye of a studio.)

For novelists, this is a worthy world to dive into as well. They may find ideas they can be passionate about that will take half the work of an original novel. They have a better chance of their novelizations landing on the big screen. They have a shot at better sales if any of those novels are made into films and the novelizations rerelease with the movie posters on the front. All of this helps novelists become more visible in the film industry; it may call the attention of studios, networks, and producers to their other books. Can you say win-win?

For novelists and screenwriters, for producers and publishers, there is no downside to playing in this creative world. (So, why didn't we think of this sooner?)

What You Will Learn in This Book

There are many questions surrounding this creative arena that we will discuss in this book. For example, how does a novelist know which stories to take on and which projects to avoid? Why is it important to not change everything the screenwriter wrote? And yet, how flexible does the screenwriter need to be when watching someone else adapt (read: change) his words?

Screenwriters, we will help you understand why the novelist will have to make some changes to your beloved, original story, its structure, its dialogue, and other areas in the translation to book form. We will also share some tips on how to make sure you are working with a team that actually wants to adapt *your* story.

There are patterns we have picked up on that have become helpful to recognize as we approach each novelization. Some key questions we will answer are:

- What makes it easier to write these books over novels written from scratch?

- What are the challenges of novelizations?

- What's important to keep, to expand, or throw away from the original script's story?

- If the screenwriter is not writing the novelization, how involved should that screenwriter be with the novelist?

- What's the best way to form a partnership between screenwriters and novelists?

- What changes should screenwriters be flexible on and what should they fight for?

We will answer these and many other questions throughout this book.

And here's the cool part. Since collectively, we have done this on seven projects so far, we have specific examples from our own published work plus a few works-in-progress. You will get the chance to compare side-by-side script pages to the novelization pages that followed. We will explain our whole process: why certain parts of the novel are faithful to the script and why other parts veer off in different directions. We will show you how each writing arena follows different rules and how to use the tools unique to novelists in the novelization process.

For those screenwriters who are also aspiring novelists, there is so much you must learn to do your own adaptations. It's like having to rewire your brain to think the *exact opposite* to how it functioned when you penned your screenplay. We will also give you short exercises in select chapters to put what you're learning into practice.

We will cover such topics as setting, length, point of view, backstory, interior monologue, and the translation of dialogue, character, and structure from script-to-book.

And just a quick word about the format of this book. It's not that we love seeing our names and titles in print.

Since this book is co-written by a screenwriter and a novelist, we will label each section for you, so you know who is speaking. This way you'll know if you are being given advice from the screenwriter's POV or the novelist's POV, or which one of us is doing the comparison from script to novel. Just because we don't want to be completely annoying with agreement problems by always having to qualify a writer in the singular as a "he or she," we will often refer to one as a "she." We mean no disrespect to the wonderful male authors and screenwriters out there. (Rock on, Bill Myers, James Scott Bell, Tom Clancy, Nicholas Sparks!)

Are you ready to dive in with us, into this new, exciting, creative world?

Chapter Two
CHANGES & CHALLENGES

Cheryl McKay (aka The Screenwriter)

Changes, Changes, Changes

Dearest Screenwriters: I know. Our writing is precious. We wrote every word perfectly, so why does it have to change?

You know I'm kidding about perfection. However, if we didn't like what we wrote, we wouldn't have committed those words to paper. (At least not by the "rewritten twenty times over" draft we're willing to show a novelist or publisher to be considered for publication!) So why is it important that we be open to changes when it comes to the adaptations of our scripts into novels? What should we be flexible on? Which battles are worth fighting?

Learning what novelists go through in penning novelizations and what tools they have unique to their writing form will give you a deeper appreciation for what they do. It will show you that what works in a script doesn't always work in book form. If you work hard to understand the process, you will find yourself much more flexible to work with and perhaps form an alliance that could benefit you for years to come. This book will help you grasp the differences in our writing mediums, perhaps equipping you to also consider doing your own novelizations. (Then when you make changes, you can blame yourself and understand what a novelist faces!)

If you have ever adapted a book into a screenplay, you already know how much has to change from that novelist's book to translate the same story to the big screen. You know how flexible that author has to be for her book to get adapted. And let's admit it: other than someone on the level of J.K. Rowling, that author most often will have no choice or power or even involvement in the process. So this is the reverse. If you are not doing your own novelization, the shoe gets to be on the other foot—yours. You get to watch someone else take your work and do her own translation of it.

Your novelist is going to need the same flexibility, understanding, and grace when it comes to adjustments needed to your work. If you are not flexible, you might as well get out of the novelization business (or the writing business in general).

What has to change is going to be different for every project. Each script will need to be evaluated individually. Rene can speak to what changed the most in her projects with other screenwriters and she will walk you through examples. For the work jointly between us, we have noticed predictable patterns. Story, structure, characters, dialogue, and voices tend to be the areas that need the least amount of changes from my scripts to novels. However, the need for having point of view character(s), a lot more backstory, interior monologue, and details about setting tend to be where the most changes or additions have been. Each of these topics will have their own chapter ahead, as we dig deeper.

Keep this in mind: if something changes in your book that you don't like, it doesn't mean it's going to end up in a movie if your script gets made later. You don't have to change your script to match the book. You may have to face a producer reading the book version and wanting that story change added to your script, but you don't have to make that change voluntarily.

Sometimes, you may like a change for the sake of the book but don't feel like it's necessary for the film version.

Let me share one example from *Never the Bride*: I wrote a sequence where Jessie goes speed dating on Valentines Day. Because we wanted to shoot the production on a lower budget, I let Jessie have all the dialogue in that sequence and just visually showed the variety of men she sat down with at the tables. I show their types visually rather than by what comes out of their mouths. In a book, you can't depend on those visual cues. Rene had great fun blowing that scene up—introducing the variety of men—letting them talk, finding voices for each. She even found a funny pay off to a guy Jessie had seen in a prior scene. I chose not to add all of these speaking characters into my script, even though the sequence is funnier in the book. This was a choice based on the realities of the film business and its costs, not because the scene wasn't better in book form.

Novelists can give dialogue to anyone they want to and it doesn't cost any more than the ink on the page. Yet for every actor who speaks on camera, we have to provide higher payments and future residuals. If an "extra" doesn't speak, we can pay less and avoid residuals. So in script form, I stuck with the montage, letting Jessie do all the talking. This also saved me about four script pages, which would have also made it more costly to shoot. The book is more fun; the script is written in a more cost-effective way for the medium and moves the story forward a bit faster. Yet, the heart of the scene is the same. I didn't feel like Rene's adds were in any way a departure from the heart of my story; I enjoyed her expansion of it.

On the other hand, if something gets added to the book that you love, depending on how you do your contracts, you may be able to add that into your script and make your script better.

The Need for More Words
Besides the fact that scripts and books are different writing mediums, some changes are necessary because of the need for length. The interior monologue and backstory are two

great areas for a novelist to expand the length through the narrative. Each project starts with an assignment of the book length by the publisher. A novelist needs to know this information to know how much expansion will be necessary. (When independently publishing, the authors will need to predetermine their target word count so they have an understanding of how much expansion they'll need.) There is a big difference in the word count of a script vs. the word count of a novel.

The feature film that I wrote, *The Ultimate Gift*, was based on a novel by Jim Stovall. As mentioned, once we shot the film version, Thomas Nelson Publishers wanted to partner with the production company on a novella that matched the film version of the story to release with the film. Because they decided they wanted it to be an extremely close match to the script, a full-length novel could not be written. Rene did not have the freedom to add much backstory or characters that weren't pre-established in the script, or use the expansion tools a novelist would normally have.

The publisher ordered a novella of 40,000 words. The script was just over 20,000 words. So the need for expansion was far less than most of the other projects we do. Rene and I did not know each other yet and did not work on *The Ultimate Gift* together. She only had my script from which to work. There were many times she wished she had access to me to ask questions. Thankfully, once we formed our partnership for future projects, we've been able to work together. We will discuss how to form the most beneficial partnerships between screenwriters and novelists in the final chapter.

Ironically, the only scene Rene was able to add to *The Ultimate Gift* novella that wasn't in the script was a scene I had in an early draft of my script. She never saw that scene nor heard about. She just used her writer instincts and added a scene that was one of my long lost favorites, gone before we shot the film. When I read the novella, I knew this was a writer who was on my page, who closely matched the style and heart of the way I love to write. That is when our partnership began.

When we got our contract for *Never the Bride*, the assignment was to write an 80,000-word novel based on a 22,000-word script. That's a far greater difference in length than *The Ultimate Gift*. The chapters ahead will discuss what tools the novelist has to expand and how to get that word count up. We will show examples and discuss some of the changes that had to take place to make it long enough.

One last word about length: just because a novel needs more words than a script does not mean it has filler. There is a bigger art to it than just adding words. They need to evoke emotions, interestingly convey new or fresh information, and draw in the reader. They need to take over the role of what an actor could do on screen but with words. This is no easy task. This is why sometimes it's best to partner with someone who knows what she's doing or get trained yourself so you can do your own novelizations.

A Word to the Novelist

You have to remember if you are adapting a script into a novel, you don't want to just make it your own and not respect the work of the screenwriter. Changing everything will undermine the point of the process and will double your workload (probably for half the pay). If that screenwriter doesn't recognize the story when you and your publisher finish with it, don't expect her to go out cheerleading the novel when trying to set up the screenplay as a film or TV series. The screenwriter is likely going to want to get her own script made into a film, not the version you came up with, unless the screenwriter agreed to the changes and was part of that overhaul.

One battle screenwriters fight when getting a film made is everyone wants to "put their stamp" on their project and make it their own. This means often, once a film gets made, it's unrecognizable to the original writer. Yes, this is frustrating. When it comes to the novelist's role, I strongly suggest you not tackle a project in a way that tries to make it your own or make changes just for the sake of change. Only make changes that are right for the story and the book medium. Choose to get involved because you like the story, not because you are out to change it.

So far, Rene and I haven't had any of those battles on our projects. Our partnership has been great. The only change battle for one of our projects was one we fought together over a proposed title change. The publisher, in-house, had renamed the book version of one of my scripts into a different title and had been calling it that for months before they mentioned it to us. But this title—while cute—was not a title I could ever use for the film. Their new title would have limited my market. Rene and I requested they consider leaving the title the same. We had to alert the publisher if they changed it and a movie got made, we'd never be able to release the film with the same title. It would lose its easy cross-promotion. It could have compromised their ability to sell a lot more books upon the movie's release when it would be harder to make sure the public knew it was the same story. Thankfully, the publisher was generously open to our concerns and let us keep the title. It wouldn't have been the first time a book title didn't match a film, but let's be honest. Fans of Nicholas Sparks' *The Notebook: a novel* are much more likely to notice a film trailer for the movie if its title is also *The Notebook*. You don't want the audience straining to figure out if the trailer is the same story under a different title.

Next I'm going to walk you through a sample where you can see a variety of changes at work in the translation from script to book.

* * *

SAMPLE A

To follow are Pages 2-4 of the *Greetings from the Flipside* screenplay.

EXT. STRIP MALL — DAY

A dress shop is nestled between stores.

INT. DRESS SHOP — DAY

Hope shakes her hands up and down, working out her nervous energy, as BECCA, 30s, her loyal, married, pregnant friend, zips up the back of Hope's wedding dress. A SEAMSTRESS checks the length of the hem.

> BECCA
> Breathe, Hope.

> HOPE
> Looks like someone threw
> up lace.

Hope breathes oddly. Becca hugs her from behind.

> BECCA
> Oh, Sweetie, you look
> beautiful.

> HOPE
> You're wrinkling it.

> SEAMSTRESS
> Hem looks good.

> HOPE
> (breathes oddly)
> I'm fine. Nobody panic.
> Just ignore the sweat.

> BECCA
> You and Sam love each other.
> Why are you panicking?

```
                    HOPE
          Who's panicking? I'm simply
          hyperventilating. Loving
          someone... it's not that
          much of a risk. I mean,
          32.6 percent of all marriages
          survive beyond the seventh
          year.
               (to the seamstress)
          Sam sang me this song.
          If only you could hear it...
          although you don't want me to
          sing it for you. Trust me.
               (nerves overtake her)
          Oh, no!
```

She races for the bathroom.

```
                  SEAMSTRESS
          Not on the dress!  Is
          she pregnant?
```

EXT. NURSING HOME - DAY - ESTABLISHING

ELDERLY PEOPLE sit in wheelchairs on the
lawn, doing nothing.

INT. NURSING HOME — PATIENT ROOM - DAY

Hope, in uniform, wheels a laundry cart into
a room. She stops at the door where towels
are on the floor. Throws them in her cart.

She peeks in the room. It's lived in but
empty at the moment. The dresser near the
door sports lots of bereavement cards. She
picks up the one in front, reads:

THERE ARE FIVE STAGES OF GRIEF. Inside, it
says: LET THE LORD HELP YOU THROUGH EACH
STAGE, ONE STEP AT A TIME.

Hope smiles mischievously, grabs a pen, crosses out the inside line and writes her own revision: YOU'VE BEEN IN DENIAL FOR A WHILE. CAN I HELP YOU MOVE ON TO ANGER?

She giggles, enjoying her own wacked sense of humor. Puts the revised card back on the dresser.

REVEAL: cards behind it have already received her revisions.

INT. NURSING HOME - GRANDMOTHER'S ROOM - DAY

Hope's GRANDMOTHER, 90, mindlessly rocks in a wheelchair.

Hope straightens a crease in the bedspread. The nightstand displays several handmade cards from Hope.

                    GRANDMOTHER
          Thank you, young lady.

                    HOPE
          It's me, Grandma.

                    GRANDMOTHER
          Okay.

The woman twirls a Columbine flower in her hand.

                    HOPE
          Guess what, Grandma? It's
          happening this weekend.
          Finally.

                    GRANDMOTHER
          Okay.

INT. NURSING HOME - COMMON ROOM - DAY

The ELDERLY are scattered throughout the room. Hope comes in wheeling a laundry cart. MISS GERTIE, 70s, approaches. She TALKS LOUDLY because she's hard-of-hearing.

          MISS GERTIE
     We are so happy it's your
     last day!

Miss Gertie gives the perplexed Hope a hug. MRS. TEASLEY, 80s, joins in.

          MRS. TEASLEY
     So happy, my dear. So
     happy.

Both ladies release her and catch her hurt expression.

          MRS. TEASLEY (CONT'D)
     But don't you worry. You'll
     be invited back here one day
     when you're a widow like us.

Hope breathes in nervously, the comment about loss affecting her. Miss Gertie pulls Hope to a couch.

          MISS GERTIE
     Now you come over here. We
     need to have a chat. I know
     this comes as a startle. But
     when you get married, you're
     going to have duties.

          HOPE
       (pales)
     We really don't have to talk.

                    MISS GERTIE
Doesn't take long. You
just endure it.
        (pats Hope's knee)
I bet you'll be pregnant
by Christmas.

                    HOPE
Will you make sure my grandma
gets a fresh flower every day?
Since Sam and I are moving to
New York City, I can't come
very often.

                    MISS GERTIE
Only if, when you find that
job making your own greeting
cards, you send me a new card
every day. They sure do make
me giggle.

                    HOPE
I promise.

                    * * *

To follow is the opening scene of *Greetings from the Flipside: a novel*: (approx. 6 novel pages)

"Suck it in. Come on, suck it in."

"My stomach is on the other side of my spine," Hope wheezed, barely enough air in her lungs to finish the sentence. Becca tugged and jiggled the zipper while trying to maintain a smile for the crowd of elderly residents who'd gathered around for the fitting. Normally Hope would be leading them into the bingo hall, but today was different. Special. There was a certain excitement on all the faces of those who'd managed to stay conscious. "Are you sure you gave them the right measurements?" Hope whispered to Becca.

"Are you sure you haven't been eating cheese? Or Popsicles? Both?"

Then, with one final tug, the zipper slid up the teeth and the dress closed. Hope let out the breath she was holding, her stomach pooching a little. She prayed she wouldn't blow the seams out.

She turned and smiled for her seamstresses, every one of which was in a wheelchair or held steady by a walker.

"Oh, honey!" Mrs. Teasley gasped. "It looks beautiful. You're stunning!"

Miss Gertie, who had worked as a seamstress her whole life, wheeled closer. "Did you notice the hem, Hope? It's done the old-fashioned way. These days, nobody takes time on the hem, rushing through it as if it doesn't matter. It is the most important part!"

"Miss Gertie, it's perfect." Hope whirled around, glancing in the mirror they'd brought out for her. She'd been hesitant when the nursing-home gang offered to make her dress. But she was barely making over minimum wage here, and her mother certainly didn't have any money to help. It had been a gamble, and for once, she won.

Mr. Collins's hearing aid went off, sounding like a dying fire alarm. "Mr. Collins!" Hope tapped on her ear to let him know. She twirled again, her fingers sweeping over the hand-stitched pearls and the lace on the sleeves.

"Sam will love me no matter what I look like," she said to Becca. "But I look awfully good, don't I?"

Becca clapped. Miss Gertie wheeled even

closer to Hope. "I'm so glad this is your last day."

Hope laughed. "I know you mean that in the nicest way."

"You're too good for this place. You've got to go out in this world, make a name for yourself!"

That was the plan, to flee Poughkeepsie and move to New York City with Sam right after the wedding. She'd dreamed of it her whole life, and it was almost here. She glanced at Miss Gertie and Mrs. Teasley, both of whom had their hands clasped together, pure delight shining in their eyes.

Hope leaned in for hugs. "I'm going to miss you both."

Miss Gertie sat up a little straighter in her chair. "Listen, we need to talk."

"About what?"

"I know this may come as a startle, but when you get married, you're going to have duties."

It was something about the way she said *duties* under her breath that made Hope realize Miss Gertie wasn't talking about vacuuming. "We don't really need . . . we don't have to talk."

"Doesn't take long, dearie." Mrs. Teasley patted her hand. "Just endure it."

"I bet she'll be pregnant by Christmas!" Miss Gertie said to the room full of hearing aids. At the word *pregnant* seven of the ten ladies woke to attention. Ms. Cane was looking at her own belly.

A hot flush crept up Hope's neck. "Miss Gertie, really, it's okay —"

Suddenly Mr. Snow shuffled in, moving faster than anyone on a walker should. His bright white hair was blown back and he leaned way forward on his walker, making him look like he was fighting a stiff north wind. Hope knew he was looking for her but probably wasn't recognizing her in the long, white dress.

"Mr. Snow, over here!"

"Ah! There you are. Didn't see you." He shuffled her way, smiling, his always-clean dentures sparkling under the fluorescent lights. He let go of his walker, which normally didn't turn out well for him, and grabbed her hand as he wobbled. "I'm going to miss you, Hopeful."

"I'm going to miss you too, Snowball."

He reached into the small bag that hung off the side of his walker and pulled out a card. "I couldn't let you leave without giving you a card to rewrite."

Hope read it aloud. "'There are five stages of grief.'" Hope looked at Mr. Snow. "I'm sorry. Who died?"

"My cousin, Burt. He was one hundred and three years old and wanted to die two decades ago."

"Ah." Hope opened the card. "'Let the Lord help you with each stage, one step at a time.'"

Mr. Snow took out a pen from his bag and handed it to her. Hope thought for a moment, then scratched out the fancy italics, wrote beside them, then handed the card back to Mr. Snow. He slid his reading glasses on. "'There are five stages of grief.'" His shaky hand opened the card. "'You've been in denial for a while. Can I help you move on to anger?'"

The room was suddenly quiet. Hope fidgeted . . . too snarky? Too insensitive?

Then Mr. Snow threw his head back and laughed. Everyone else joined in and soon the room was filled with chuckles. Mr. Snow slapped her on the back. "Good one."

Becca looked at her. "We're going to have to go soon."

Hope nodded. She knew it was time to say her good-byes. One by one, she bent down to hug each person, careful to avoid any mishaps with the dress. Some of them hugged back. Some of them didn't. But they all knew she loved them.

She made her way to Miss Gertie and knelt by her wheelchair. "Will you make sure my grandmother's fresh flower arrives every day?"

"Only if, when you find that job making your own greeting cards, you send me a new card every day. They sure do make me giggle."

"I promise."

Becca tapped her watch. "We've got about forty more things to do today."

"Just a few more minutes." Hope hiked her dress up to her shins, headed down Wing Two. She smiled and nodded at all the familiar faces: Mr. Speigel, a once-successful CEO for a large bank, who hadn't had a single visitor in the last four years; Aunt Jackie, as she liked to be called, who suffered a stroke in September and lost the ability to move any muscles in her face— but there was life in those green eyes of hers; Old Benny, once a major-league baseball player, now with amputations at both knees because of diabetes. He lost his sight and his mind back in '08.

The door to Hope's grandmother's room was open, like always. Two towels were tossed on the floor. Hope dutifully stooped to pick them up and throw them in the hamper. Her grandmother sat by the window, staring out at nothing more than an empty lot washed in hazy sunlight, twirling a Columbine flower in her hand.

Hope scooped up tissues, flattened the silky bedspread, fluffed the pillows, wiped clean the sink, and replaced the tissue box. Five cards lined the same table that held the tissues. Ten more sat across Grandmother's nightstand, and another ten on the cabinet. There were weeks when Hope wrote a card a day and brought them to her grandmother's room. Sometimes they didn't move, other times her grandmother would give them away or, when she was more lucid, mail them. Mostly they just sat with all the others, simply signed *Hope*. A glance at one of the wittier lines she wrote caused her to laugh, and her grandmother looked her way.

"Thank   you,   young   lady."   Her grandmother's smile, though feeble, was gentle and genuine. She didn't seem to take notice of the long, white dress Hope wore.

Hope   stooped   by   her   wheelchair. "Grandma, it's me."

"Okay."

"I wanted you to see me in my dress. It's finally happening. This weekend."

"Okay."

"I wish you could be there, but I know you'll be there in your heart."

"Okay."

"Did I tell you that Sam is writing me a song? I probably did. He's been writing it for a long time. I thought he was going to have it ready at Christmas, but he said he needed a little more time. He hasn't said it, but I'm pretty sure he's going to debut it at the wedding. I heard he's been inquiring about getting a grand piano into the church." The thought made her smile. She'd been dying to hear the song, imagining it over and over in her head. "So, Grandma, Sam and I are moving to New York City. That's right.

I'm finally getting out of Poughkeepsie, just like you always wanted." Hope paused, searching the elderly woman's eyes. She laughed at the memory of her grandmother, before she lost her mind, trying to talk her into some boy from Hope's school days. "I have a feeling about him," she would say.

Cheryl McKay (aka The Screenwriter)

Changes Comparison (Sample A)
The sample from the script was 629 words, 3 pages. The novel version was: 1511 words, 6 pages

Let's look at some of the changes that took place to write this translation. While it can be easy to crosscut and jump locations in a film (and we depend on those visuals), Rene decided to streamline those opening scenes by moving Hope's dress fitting scene to the nursing home. She made one of the old ladies the seamstress. This helped us settle into one place, gave us more time to get to know the people in the nursing home, and enjoy a longer scene. Creatively, it was a great choice as well.

Rene allowed Hope to rewrite Mr. Snow's card on the spot in the common area of the nursing home, rather than in a scene by herself like I had in the script. Rene colored in fun details about the nursing home, who the people were, slices of their backgrounds, how they play bingo, and other specifics I didn't need in the script.

As the screenwriter, it was nice to see some of the dialogue preserved. But Rene also finessed what she needed to, to make the new structure work, and wrote new dialogue to fit the setting change for the dress fitting. She also got the chance to tell you more about Hope's dreams upon going to New York City, information that comes out in later script scenes.

As the screenwriter, I could see how any changes made enhanced the novel version. Yet, it wasn't such a departure from my work that I felt like I was reading a different story. Rene also added lots of humor. In the section I wrote about "duties" where a lot of dialogue is preserved, Rene got to add the hilarious interior monologue that said, "Miss Gertie wasn't talking about vacuuming." What great humor that gave the scene from her internal thoughts, and it was consistent with Hope's voice.

Rene also chose to reverse the order of the scenes so we meet the grandmother after the scene with the older ladies. This is a lovely change so she can show her grandmother what she looks like in her wedding dress. Rene still included my scene where she goes to talk to her, but it has more color and richness to it. You will get to see the rest of that scene in the setting chapter, where Rene continued with my dialogue but also weaved in wonderful details about the setting.

* * *

Rene Gutteridge (aka The Novelist)

Worth the Change?
Because novelizations are becoming more popular, novelization opportunities are increasing. Many of my novelist friends have gotten offers for or have been inquiring into the possibilities of novelizations.

There are many points a novelist should consider before taking on a project. Because all novels are such big undertakings, there are important questions every novelist should ask herself before agreeing to do the adaptation. To follow are some questions to ponder:

> **1. Am I excited about this project?** Whether you are paid to write the novelization or writing it on spec (meaning you do the work beforehand in hopes of selling it afterward), you must really like the project. You're going to spend hours, days, weeks, months with these characters, plots, and

dialogue. If you're bored out of your mind reading the script, you're going to struggle to bring any enthusiasm to the plate.

2. How much research will this take? One of the vast differences between a script and a book is the information. For instance, a script can simply say in a heading: <u>France, 1792</u>. It's up to other people — the director, production designers, costumers — to create France in 1792. Not so for the novelist. If you're going to write a scene or a book set in France in 1792 then you're going to have to know 1792 France like the back of your hand. A sci-fi script, for example, would require great detail from the writer about the world that has been created. You have someone running an ad agency? You're going to need to know the ins and outs of that world. If the lead character in the script is a bee keeper, be prepared to learn a lot! All of this is because of the nature of novel writing. The novelist is solely responsible for all the information that needs to be there to tell the story. The great thing is that most novelists are so curious that we enjoy learning about new worlds. Just make sure the subject is interesting enough for you to do the research.

3. Do I like the screenwriter? This question applies if you're in a collaborative situation with the screenwriter. I've worked on projects where I was hired to adapt a script without working with the writer. I did, however, work with the producers. If you are working with the screenwriter, you need to talk extensively with her and fully explain the adaptation process. I have found most screenwriters are extremely generous in this area, Cheryl being a prime example. I think this is because screenwriters are used to their work being interpreted by vast amounts of people.

4. Will I be fairly compensated? The question of who gets paid and how much should be worked out before the process begins. I've not found this to be a problem so far, but don't begin anything until you've clearly outlined a collaborative agreement between yourself and the screenwriter (and the publisher, if applicable).

5. Are there extensive story holes or other problematic elements to the script? If there are, this doesn't mean you should dismiss the script altogether. But you do have to understand that if there are story holes to fill, you'll be the one to do it. And sometimes these can be complicated. One of the things I've appreciated about Cheryl's scripts is how strong they are by the time I read them. You'll want to consider a script that has gone through many drafts, as opposed to a script that's hot off its first draft. The script literally needs to stand on its own or you're going to get more work than you bargained for. Typically novelizations are less work for novelists because it's as if you're working from a very detailed outline. So keep in mind, for everything you're going to need to fix (story structure, timeline problems, etc.), that is more time you'll spend working on the project. Only you can decide if it will be worth the effort. Occasionally, these adaptations become difficult no matter how strong the script is. It usually has to do with the entire adaptation process, not necessarily a weak script.

6. Does this story lend itself to novel form? There are certain genres that are harder to write than others. A script filled with a ton of action or slapstick comedy will be a more difficult adaptation. Likewise, a script with little movement (for example, it all takes place in a warehouse) can also be challenging.

7. Is the script a genre you are comfortable writing? The novelist needs to consider her own talents and writing tastes. If you typically write romance and you've got an action-comedy on your hands, take that into account when making your decision.

Challenges Novelists Face in Translation

There are patterns we've picked up on that screenwriters use a lot in script form that do not translate well into novels. They are:

- Short Scenes or Montages
- Flashbacks
- Crosscutting
- Voice-over
- Physical Comedy

Because of the nature of film—which is told visually and audibly—there are many facets of scriptwriting that will never translate well. I run into these in every novelization that I do. Typically they're easily fixable, by taking the *purpose* of the untranslatable scene and making sure that the reason it's there is shown in another way that works better.

First, let's look at the problem of short scenes. In *The Ultimate Gift*, there was a short scene in which the main character is being chased by a dog. In all, the scene probably lasted less than ten seconds on screen and was part of a montage sequence. Because the people involved with the project wanted all scenes in as much as possible, I tacked that scene onto a larger scene, which sequentially made sense in both the book and movie. Short scenes are usually not difficult to deal with. If these little snippets, which cause a movie to flow well and keep up the pace, are essential for the story, make it the middle of a scene and then add front end and back end story to it. You're simply expanding the scene. Unfortunately in novels, you rarely see a short scene, like half a page. Sometimes it's done for effect, but mostly you just don't see it.

Flashbacks are another challenge. In novels alone, they can be challenging. But as they're used in scripts, they're particularly hard because often they're shown very fast. In a novelization I did with director John Ward called *Heart of the Country*, the script called for multiple flashbacks, where two characters are thinking back on how they fell in love. Visually, these were beautiful flashbacks and I wanted to keep them. So in the first draft of the novel, I tried to write them in and stay as close as possible to the script.

Yet upon conferring with my editors, we quickly realized that it simply didn't work to keep going back into the past while trying to move the story forward. Ultimately, we chose to keep the storyline of how they met, but we moved it to the beginning and told the story sequentially. The flashbacks worked wonderfully in the script, and the sequential ordering of the scenes worked just as well in the novel. Both managed to tell the same story in the way that best fit each form.

Crosscut sequences are another challenge, but again can be modified fairly easily by stringing all the pieces of the crosscuts into one scene. The idea in a novel is to expand the scene. So let's say you have in a script scenes that go back and forth between two people having a conversation. In novel form, you have to pick which character to tell that scene through (POV) and stick with that character. Novels can run scenes simultaneously, but it's done in a different way than in a script. Each scene must completely stand on its own and have its own, stable purpose, which typically means scenes will be longer than short crosscuts.

Voice-overs can't be used very well. Sometimes they can be folded into first-person narration, but typically they're not usable in novel format. An exception to this rule is using a prologue to set up a character's voice. But a prologue by nature is set apart from the rest of the book, so the voice-over narrative must be compelling enough to stand on its own.

Regarding physical comedy, in *Never the Bride*, Cheryl had written a funny scene where the character Jessie runs and falls into a fountain. This may seem like a perfectly acceptable scene, and it is for film. But trying to write physical comedy in a novel can be challenging. It's not impossible, but mostly what is funny in novels are dialogue and interior monologue. *Showing* a girl topple into a fountain is hilarious. Describing it to a reader is difficult. So in that particular place in the script, I wrote a different scenario, which accomplished the same thing but was told differently. The entire intent of the scene was still there.

Novelists can typically feel their way through these processes and decide what can be saved and what must be tossed. Whether a scene is cut or kept, it's always important for the novelist to recognize *why* a certain scene is in the script so she can capture its purpose in the novel.

In the next chapter, we will look at setting and how it can bring your novel life.

Chapter Three

SETTING

Cheryl McKay (aka The Screenwriter)

Lights, Camera, Setting

We've all seen movies that have wowed us with their visuals, how specifically everything was chosen, from the sets, to the props, to the costumes, all serving the time period and the visual look of the film. (They give away Oscars to those who do this well.)

There are many departments whose jobs contribute to the setting of the film. The camera department, the production designer, crewmembers who work in locations, art direction, set building, props, wardrobe.

The location department finds the best places to shoot, which will fit the time period and the style of the film. They consider the locations the screenwriter suggested through their slug lines. (Example: INT. DINER – NIGHT.) Set decorators can turn a modern room into a 1970s throwback with the right furniture, artwork, rugs, lamps, etc. The wardrobe department finds the right costumes, shoes, jewelry, head dressings. The make up and hair department create the right looks for the actors.

Screenwriters do not have to write those details into the script; they leave a lot of this work up to those capable crewmembers. If a screenwriter gets too detailed, the reader will probably get annoyed with him! So much of this visual detail gets discovered in making the film, not the moment the ideas were penned to paper. A screenwriter may try to be specific on locations, like a "fifties diner" or a "lakefront property." Yet in production, many of these change based on what's available where the film shoots. (Your diner could change to an outdoor burger shack and your lakefront property may become a beachfront cottage.)

Unless a story must take place in one location or region only, it can be beneficial for a script to not be so tied to one area. This is because where the film shoots will often depend on who picks up a script for production and what the funding source is, which states are currently offering the best incentives. For example, if your funding group comes from Virginia with the directive that you shoot in their home state, your Boston, Massachusetts, set story will be rewritten to suit the location.

What a Novel Setting!
Novels need descriptions of setting elements that go far beyond what any script should contain. They need to be specific. Novelists should paint a picture for the reader—even if the location is fictional. Coloring in setting details is one of the fun parts of novel writing. It's like the novelist gets to take on the job of the production designer of a film and paint in specifics that won't be in the script.

When we wrote *Never the Bride*, my original script took place in Santa Barbara, so Rene used that location for the novel. The script has since been changed to a generic southern beach town since we are considering four different states for the film shoot.

Before we show you a sample of how setting works in a script-to-novel adaptation, I'll share my experience when writing my novelization of my script *Song of Springhill*. I wrote a screenplay based on the mining disasters of the fifties that happened in Springhill, Nova Scotia: a large explosion in 1956 that killed 39 men, and the 1958 "Bump" (underground earthquake) that killed 75. My grandfather was trapped in the mines during the Bump and missed the Explosion by only a few hours. One of my favorite parts of writing that script was coming up with details from the fifties time period. Because it's inspired by actual events, keeping the original time period and location were important. Yet the details required in script form pale in comparison to the novel.

In the script, when describing details within a scene, I could be generic. For example, my script could include in the action line, "It's Christmas Eve and the family decorates the tree." However, when I was writing the novel version, I knew that information was far too generic to be interesting to a novel reader. So I researched the question: what did Christmas ornaments look like in 1956? In the script form, you can easily let the art department track down the right kinds of ornaments from 1956. But in novel form, it's worth looking into what ornaments were around so you can include details in the scene description.

During a pool hall scene, I wrote, "He sinks a pool ball." When I wrote the novel version, I wondered if those pool balls looked the same as we know them today. Were they colored and striped? Numbered? In a script, who cares? But in a novel, it matters. Sometimes, the more specific you get in a novel, the more interesting it is to read. So I researched vintage pool balls so I could include the correct details. As a screenwriter-turned-novelist in that moment, I had a blast coloring in details that I usually breeze over.

In script form, I quoted lyrics from fifties songs that I'd like a production company to consider using in the film. However, you can't just put those into a book because lyrics are copyrighted. You can put them in an unpublished script (though it's suggested you do so sparingly) because the assumption is either the production will pay for the rights to use them — if they like your song choices — or they will choose something else. In a novel, you can't use lyrics unless you get permission or pay for the rights. Most novelists don't want to track down who owns the rights to Elvis's *HeartBreak Hotel* or the Everly Brother's *Wake Up Little Susie* because it would cost way too much to include either one. Titles supposedly are not copyrightable, so in book form, I have mentioned song titles.

Let's review: setting encompasses locations, props, costumes, and the time period, including historical events if it's a period piece. If you are doing the novelization, pay attention to all of these areas and see how you can strengthen the read through your descriptions of them.

* * *

Rene Gutteridge (aka The Novelist)

Hot Tips on Setting
When I was working with John Ward on *Heart of the Country,* it was helpful to me that John had lived in both of the settings of the novel: North Carolina and New York City. There were little details he gave me that I wouldn't have known without a great deal of research. For example, I wrote a scene with an old gravel road that led up to a house. When John was reviewing the book, he let me know that in that region of North Carolina, the gravel would be made of seashells. It was a great piece of detail I immediately included.

Because the story was set on farmland, I had to dismiss my ideas of mid-western crops and research what was grown in that part of the country. As Cheryl mentioned, these details are a part of why it takes so long to write a novel. The novelist must bring the reader into the world, one detail at a time.

So, here are some things to consider when working with setting:

- Understand the world about which you are writing. Read about it. Research it. Go there if you can. I even use Google Earth to "fly" to a place I want to write about.

- Less is more. Readers don't need a boatload of detail. They need the details that matter. A few interesting details are way more engaging than an abundance of dull facts that don't mean anything to the story. If you're going to describe the wallpaper, there should be a good reason.

- Setting doesn't have to be at the front of your chapters. Sprinkle it in as part of the fabric of the story. Scripts always start with setting but novels don't have to.

* * *

SAMPLE B

To follow is one brief scene from Cheryl's script *Greetings from the Flipside*. This scene was included to set up the location, what's often in scripts called the "Establishing Shot":

```
EXT.   POUGHKEEPSIE,   NEW   YORK   -   DAY   -
ESTABLISHING

The city bordered by the Hudson River holds
thirty thousand people stretched across 5.7
square   miles.   Some   call   it   historic,
colonial;  others  see  its  lack  of  progress.
Life seems a bit grey here, foggy.  Lacking
in true color.
```

* * *

To follow is a scene from *Greetings from the Flipside* novel, a continuation of the sample from the prior chapter. This includes the segment used to introduce the setting:

But Grandma also always wanted bigger and better for Hope, and everyone knew bigger and better was not to be found in Poughkeepsie. The name itself implied its own identity crisis. Few knew how to even pronounce the name and those in the know disagreed as to whether it was *puh* or *poo* or *poe*. The *kips-see* was generally acknowledged by all as the proper way to end the word, but then there was the question as to whether Poughkeepsie was upstate or downstate. Also in question was the matter of the town and the city. For no reason anyone could identify, Poughkeepsie was split into the *Town* of Poughkeepsie and the *City* of Poughkeepsie. The town boasted enormous houses and even larger taxes. The city had low taxes and lower housing.

To grow up in the Spackenkill District was to go to its privileged high school, where lockers didn't even need locks. Hope did not live near nor even infrequently visit that district, but overall Poughkeepsie was a decent place to grow up, with a glorious view of the Hudson at dusk. The smog did wonders for the color spectrum. It was home to Vassar College and the Culinary Institute of America and city-dwellers were flocking to Poughkeepsie, pushing the population over thirty-five thousand.

She looked out the window her grandmother stared out of every day. It was a colorless view of warehouses and smokestacks. Her grandmother was born and raised here and as far as Hope was concerned, she was Poughkeepsie's shining star. But eleven major-league baseball players also hailed from Poughkeepsie, as did professional poker player Hevad Khan and the inventor of Scrabble, Alfred Mosher Butts, who sold his invention to entrepreneur James Brunot. Brunot renamed it *Scrabble*, from the Dutch word *scrabben*, meaning "to grope frantically, to scrape or scratch."

It was that word *scrabble* that defined what Hope always felt about this city and her place in it.

The word pointed her toward the escape chute, so to speak. She always felt, someday, she would make a disorderly haste straight out of this town, clambering and scraping and climbing her way to freedom.

Ironically, or perhaps not, the word was also used to mean the act or instance of scribbling or doodling and that . . . *that* . . . was her ticket out of Poughkeepsie. Simple doodling would set her free.

That, and Sam.

She turned to her grandmother, stroked her knobby shoulder with the back of her hand. "I won't be able to see you every day."

"Okay."

"But the ladies will make sure you always have a new flower. And Mom will of course come by to see you." Tears stung Hope's eyes as she looked into her grandmother's bright blue gaze, twinkling with a life Grandma no longer remembered. Hope knew — her grandmother loved this dress. Would love the wedding day if she could go, and would love Sam if she could ever know him.

A soft knock came at the door. "Hope, we have to get to the church," Becca said.

Hope squeezed the hand that didn't have the flower. "I will send you a card as soon as I get to New York City, okay?" She stood and kissed her on the cheek, which smelled like baby lotion. "I love you," Hope whispered into her ear.

"Okay."

Cheryl McKay (aka The Screenwriter)

Setting Comparison (Sample B)
The script only uses 46 words to set up the location, while in the novel, Rene had fun expanding the details of Poughkeepsie, New York, in a fun and clever way with 568

words in this sequence. It's clear she researched the area and famous people from it. There is no reason that information needs to be in a script, but it sure makes the novel a delightful read and helps us get to know the lead character through how she sees her surroundings. Hope's sense of humor comes through how Rene wrote it as well.

After establishing the setting, the rest of the scene is a continuation of the script pages from the prior chapter (Sample A). This shows the flow. Rene took the scene in the script and interrupted it with the setting details, then continued where she left off to finish the scene. Rene tied pieces of the town's details into an emotional side of the character (*scrabble*) so it wasn't just talking about a place. It tied to the story and character as well.

* * *

SAMPLE C

The next setting sample comes from Susan Rohrer's *Bright Christmas: an Amish Love Story*. Susan wrote the screenplay first, then wrote the novelization. (Used by permission.)

EXT. SMALL PENNSYLVANIA TOWN - DAY

A HORSE AND BUGGY braves MODERN TRAFFIC.

MERCHANTS festoon quaint store-fronts with pine garland and red ribbons, celebrating the yuletide season.

A LITTLE GIRL waits while her HURRIED MOM feeds a parking meter. The girl exchanges a smile with a YOUNG AMISH MAN as he tends to his RIG. Though the girl's mom urges her along, she can't help but look back and stare.

INT. PENNSYLVANIA MARKET - DAY

SHOPPERS mingle, browsing AMISH GOODS. An
OLDER WOMAN reaches for a jar of Amish-made
apple butter and examines its hand-lettered
label for the maker: CHARITY BRIGHT.

INT. BRIGHT KITCHEN - AMISH COUNTRY — DAY

Dozens of empty canning jars line the
counter in this primitive, working kitchen.
STEAM RISES from a massive kettle as apple
butter bubbles on a wood-burning stove.

An APPLE is expertly chopped, then pushed
aside into a sizeable mound.

Mature beyond her 20 years, CHARITY BRIGHT
stokes the wood stove's fire, her plain
Amish garb setting off a natural loveliness.

* * *

To follow are the opening two novel pages of *Bright Christmas*:

Charity Bright gathered firewood, her gaze drawn
to the horizon. Try as she might, she simply
couldn't shake the sensation that enveloped her.
Something was in the air. It wasn't just the scent of
fresh cut hickory and ash. No, it was far more. It
was a whisper that penetrated her being.

Change was coming.

How could something be so fearsome and yet
so fascinating? Perhaps it was because, within their
Old Order Amish district, change wasn't an
everyday — even an every year — thing. Change took
time. It meandered like the brook bordering their
property, imperceptibly carving its path. For the
most part, Charity preferred it that way. It was

comforting to know what to expect. Tomorrow would dawn soon enough.

She didn't make a fuss over birthdays, least of all her own. But this particular one—it seemed different somehow. When the sun set, then rose again, it would mean much more than simply bidding a fond farewell to her teens. There was an invisible corner she'd turn. In the morning, she'd be twenty. She'd awaken to find that the adventure of her adult life had finally begun.

Charity nestled the load of split logs into the sturdy black fabric of her everyday apron. This had been the warmest autumn in memory, so she drank in the new crispness of the air, and the Yuletide it heralded. Many favored the warmth or color of other seasons, but for Charity, there was something about the frosty Pennsylvania winters that made them the most beautiful of all. How she relished the wind's chill, the refreshing tingle against her face and hands.

She gazed at her surroundings. They had a good life. Smoke curled from the chimney of her family's wood-framed home. A light breeze dissipated the rising puffs into a brilliant blue sky. A milking cow grazed beside their red barn, the bell about her neck softly clanking with each step.

In a way, she longed to preserve it all, just as it stood, forever.

But that was not to be.

Cheryl McKay (aka The Screenwriter)

Setting Comparison (Sample C)
Isn't it interesting how different the opening images are of the script vs. the book? And yet, the same author penned both. She recognized changes were needed to write her script as a book. Both are legitimate and well done for their intended formats and audiences. For example, the script

has establishing shots in a montage format to show various parts of town. Each one establishes the Amish setting in a different way. Doing a visual-only montage (where credits would likely run) is common at the opening of a movie and helps orient viewers to the location where the story will take place. You also see how the lead character, Charity, is introduced at the end of this script montage.

But think about it: how is a novelist supposed to write a montage of images? You see the challenge? This screenwriter-turned-novelist, in the book version, wisely chose to focus on her lead character, Charity, to give us a glimpse of her internal thoughts, while giving us touches of setting. From this opening segment we know the season, the Amish setting, and we envision their life in that pastoral countryside.

When she talks about "change," she cleverly uses this as a way to bring up the brook that's bordering their property. This gives us a visual to picture for the setting while tying it to an emotional concept of how life changes a little at a time. The author sets up how idyllic Charity's life is, yet hints that change is coming, making readers want to read on to find out how her life will change.

The benefit to writing a novel is the emotion is added to the moments as we are introduced to the setting. In the script, we don't get that from the montage, but we enjoy getting that panoramic, wide-shot view first before stepping inside the lives of our characters.

Setting Exercise

Now it's your turn to look at a script page and write the first page or two of a novel. How you start a novel is extremely important. While theatergoers aren't likely to walk out of a movie during the opening credits, you may miss out on readers and book sales if your first few pages don't capture their attention. Remember: most book sellers these days show the opening pages of your novel online for free, so the readers can sample the book before they buy. So approach this assignment with that in mind.

To follow is the first page of my script, *@Malibu High*. The setting is obvious: Malibu, California. Take that one-paged segment and try your hand at the first three or four paragraphs of the novelization.

Practice painting in location details. Write how that location contrasts what's going on with the lead character and his family, having *Repo-Man* types show up to take their stuff. They are not as rich as they try to portray. This is news to the lead character, Tyler, in the opening pages.

Consider researching the area to add more details, like Rene did with *Greetings from the Flipside*. Use them to contrast the action. You could also contrast the Malibu lifestyle with valley life of Southern California since many "west-siders" (those who live closer to the ocean) look down on anyone who lives in the valley.

Even though this is a chapter on setting, keep other points in mind as you set up the opening that your reader will be asking himself about your story:

- Where am I?
- Who am I watching?
- What is the emotional situation of this character?
- Why do I care about this character?
- What questions does this opening raise?
- What questions do I want answered that make me want to keep reading?

Remember in setting up the externals — which should be painted with interesting, vivid details — you'll also want to set the emotional tone of your main character. Physical setting should be the backdrop of the emotional undertones. They should work together.

* * *

EXT. MALIBU, CALIFORNIA - DAY

RICH BRAT TEENS drive paid-for-by Daddy Jags, Beamers, and Ferraris past Malibu beaches. Recklessly. After all, they don't pay the insurance.

They belong here.

Unlike the eyesore trailing them - a beat up truck which advertises: "GIMME ALL YOUR JUNK!" It CHUGS and SPUTTERS.

So doesn't belong here.

INT. TEENAGE BOY'S BEDROOM - DAY

A Taylor guitar, played by male hands at lightning speed, finger-picking a MELODY in Eric Clapton's classic style.

EXT. MALIBU NEIGHBORHOOD - DAY

The GUITAR SOLO continues as the junk truck barrels past luxury houses arriving at...

AN EXQUISITE HOME

On the outside. Appearances can be deceiving in Malibu.

The junk truck backs up, squeezing next to the Lexus parked in the driveway. The truck uses an obnoxious BEEPER SIGNAL. It BACKFIRES as if to shout, "I'm here!"

INT. TEENAGE BOY'S BEDROOM - DAY

TYLER ZANE, 18, with a bad boy yet babyish face, continues the SOLO with his acoustic on the bed. His talent unrivaled.

An electric Fender Stratocaster leans against the wall.

A photo of Tyler being kissed by his BLONDE GIRLFRIEND is framed on the nightstand.

Lost in his own song, Tyler doesn't notice as two JUNK COLLECTORS charge his room.

The SOLO SCREECHES TO A HALT as the collectors unplug his amp. Tyler opens his eyes as they seize his stereo.

                    TYLER
          Hey!

                    * * *

Once you finish the exercise, move on to the next chapter, where Rene is going to walk you through Point of View, a concept exclusive to novelists.

Chapter Four

POINT OF VIEW

Rene Gutteridge (aka The Novelist)

Getting a Handle on POV

One of the hardest concepts to teach aspiring writers of fiction is Point of View, or POV for short. It has an entirely different meaning than in script writing, yet it is one of the most essential tools for novel writing.

Point of View is the character's view of the world. In fiction, each scene has one POV, meaning the scene is told through only one character's eyes. We see the world through him. We hear his thoughts.

There are four different types of POV in fiction: third person, first person, second person and omniscient. These may ring a bell from your childhood English classes. For our purposes, we are only going to cover first and third person, which are the two most widely used POVs.

In third person, we are given the option of changing POV, but only if a new scene begins. There is no changing POV once a scene starts. You have to stick with one character and stay with him until a scene or chapter break. Third person gives the writer the most options. Plus the viewpoint of multiple characters can be fun to play with.

Third person can contain as many or as few characters as you want, but multiple third person POV can be tricky. You don't want to use so many characters the readers have a hard time following everything. There are no general rules for how many are acceptable, but if this is your first novel, I'd say keep it to four or fewer. Two is always nice, especially for romances or good guy/bad guy scenarios. Just remember, for every character you choose to be a POV character, you must be able to get inside his head. You choose a serial killer? You'll be in his head. You have a die-hard romantic woman and you're a man? You're going to have to find your inner Nicholas Sparks. It's challenging for sure, but it is part of what makes writing in third-person such fun.

First person is perceived to be more intimate, although it is not. First person is told using "I." For example, *I walked into the store and looked around, hoping to find Eddie.* In third person, the same sentence would read, *He walked into the store and looked around, hoping to find Eddie.* First person POV follows the same rules as third, except you're telling it from one person's point of view and not multiple. First person is a difficult POV to learn. It takes a certain technique that requires a lot more study of the craft. Unless the main character is in every scene, most likely, third person is the way to go.

Whether you are in first or third person, the character can only have thoughts about what that character already knows. For example, if a meteorite is about to hit earth and your character doesn't know about it, then you can't give any hint of that meteorite hitting the earth from this character's point of view. Not until the character actually sees it with his own eyes. Maybe other characters in the book know about it, but you have to be true to what your character knows while in that POV. Here's another example. If there is a serial killer lurking in the closet and the character doesn't know it, you can't mention that killer being there until the character sees him. Remember: the reader can only experience the character's world through what he can taste, touch, hear, smell and see.

How to Switch POVs

It can be easy to slip into the error, once exploring thoughts, to share them for more than one character. But you can only do that if you switch points of view in a new chapter or sequence. You cannot go back and forth in the same scene, sharing the thoughts of more than one character. This is called head hopping. You can only see how two characters look at the same moment if part of your writing style is to repeat a scene from a different point of view in the next chapter or segment. (Ex. *Rashomon*.) But again, you still need a section break or chapter break.

It's easy to follow this rule if you change POVs at a chapter break. However, sometimes it will be necessary to change POVs within the same chapter. In a typical novel, a POV switch will be signaled by special formatting, for example, a graphical cue (i.e. dingbats, asterisks, special clip art chosen for that particular novel).

In *Greetings from the Flipside*, when we switched points of view from Jake to Hope, we used a subtitle "Greetings from My Life." These were added to help alert the reader of the POV switch.

In *Heart of the Country*, I used quite a few different POVs. So, for each chapter, I had the POV character name at the top so readers would know right off whose mind they were settling into. The last thing you want to do is confuse your readers. Following these conventions when switching POV will definitely help readers not get confused.

If you are staying in the same POV but there's been some sort of a time jump or location change within the same chapter, leave a couple of blank lines after the prior paragraph before the next paragraph begins. Don't use any special characters, like asterisks, since you are staying with the thoughts of the same POV character.

Try to stay in the same POV for at least a few pages at a time, to give your readers a chance to settle in with that character. Jumping around too often doesn't allow them to connect with that character long enough to form the attachment you want them to have.

This all may sound very technical, and experienced novelists should already know these rules. However, for the screenwriters reading this book who hope to do their own novelizations, think of these concepts as important as formatting your screenplay according to industry standards.

With all these intricate rules, POV is something that must be thoroughly studied through reading fiction and studying craft books that will go into more detail than the scope of this book. Keep in mind some famous writers in the past have ignored POV rules (ex. Agatha Christie). However, you are strongly encouraged—especially when you are first starting out—to follow POV rules.

POV as the Film Camera

I teach many classes on just POV, and I've found the most successful teaching technique is borrowed from the world of film. I have writing students hold up a pretend camera, as if they are the character they are writing. They look through the lens, which is the world from their characters' eyes. I ask them a series of questions. "Can you see the door?" *Yes.* "Can you see who is walking down the hallway?" *No.* "Can you see what the back of my shirt looks like unless I turn around?" *No.* I give them the example of a character walking into a bar, noticing a beautiful woman facing him, and the character inwardly commenting on the cute rose on the back of her jean pockets. How would he know she has a rose on her pockets? Has she turned around? Has she said she has a rose on her pocket? Unless she turns and he sees it, there is no way for him to know that. He also doesn't know who is in the bathroom or down a hallway because he just walked in. The list goes on.

Choosing POV for a Novelization

As a novelist adapting a script, the POV question is the first one that will need to be answered. The script has to be examined carefully. First and foremost, the question will be, is this first person or third person? First person is unlikely *unless* the main character is in almost every scene. The ones that she's not in cannot be used in the book, or must be modified to include her.

Early on in examining *Never the Bride*, I looked at whether it could work as first person. It seemed to be a good match for the techniques of first person. The main character was strong, opinionated and had lots of thoughts about the world. The script called for some voice-over, which also lent itself to first person. Using first person meant that some of the great scenes in the script had to be modified. It wasn't particularly hard to do.

You can easily rule out first person if there are multiple scenes that do not contain the same characters. Third person is a way more forgiving point of view. Most often, it will be the best one to serve the needs of a script adaptation. It is flexible and has the ability to set up multiple characters and scenarios and can handle the weaving of difficult plots.

Part of what we found challenging in the adaptation of Cheryl's script, *Greetings from the Flipside*, was the fact there was a big twist at the end of the movie. That twist worked great in script form. The viewer would be totally surprised and all would be well. But it didn't work in novel form because the POV character holds "the secret twist." It was challenging because technically, she doesn't know she's in a coma, so she can't convey that to the reader. But at the same time, we asked ourselves, "Can we bring the reader all the way along only to let them know none of it was happening in real life at the end?" Not certain we could chance that in book form, we decided to reveal the coma early. Whereas a film can set up visual prompts and clues (*The Sixth Sense*) a book has a much harder time concealing secrets and giving prompts in the same way. So we chose to do it in a way that helps the reader be in both worlds and understand what's going on, while also giving hints and twists along the way.

Here is another example of possibly cheating a reader and why you must carefully consider whose POV to be in, in book form. In one script of Cheryl's, she has a character who is secretly doing something to another character. In our first version of the novel, we decided to leave this character's POV out, even though he is a main character. Upon review, we decided it would be better to have him in as a POV character. Now, if we didn't adjust the text to reveal what he's doing, that would be cheating as an author. If we're in his head, we have to know what he's doing, or at the very least *hint* about what he's doing. Otherwise, you're cheating the reader.

Some adaptations are straightforward and obvious. In the novelization *Old Fashioned*, it was immediately clear there were two stories that needed to be told. It was a love story and both characters had very strong storylines, so I chose multiple third person, and used two POVs, highlighting both of the main characters.

But in *Heart of the Country*, I struggled more with how to tell this story. There were multiple characters I cared deeply about when I read the script. Their storylines were so intimate. I wanted the reader to feel close to each one. I took on the challenging task of telling the story through a rarely used technique called multiple first-person. There are very few reasons to tell a story like this, and it isn't one I'd recommend if you've never written a novel before, but for my purposes, it served me well.

Next, I'll walk you through a point of view sample from my novelization, *Old Fashioned*.

* * *

SAMPLE D

To follow is a page from the script *Old Fashioned* by Rik Swartzwelder.

INT. WORKSHOP — DAY

Dusty shafts of light through stained-glass. Antique dressers. Hand tools. Pieces of picture frames. Cans of paint and varnish-stained rags are everywhere.

A broken and very old child's rocking chair
sits in a corner with a work order tagged to
it.   HANDS gently pick up the chair, feel
its texture, select some new, matching-grain
wood.

A TABLE SAW pierces the silence. NEW BLACK-
SLOT PIECES for the rocker are cut. A LATHE
spins a NEW LEG.   SAND PAPER smoothes the
rough edges. Wider as:

CLAY WALSH double-checks his work. Clay is
in his mid-30s and on the artsy side. Messy
hair. Blue jeans. A white collared shirt,
untucked with the sleeves rolled up.

The workshop is peaceful and quiet.   The
sound of his every movement is crisp, clear.
He carefully integrates the new pieces with
the old and looks through the back slots in
the chair—like bars in a prison.

* * *

To follow is the same scene from *Old Fashioned* written in
novel form:

> His day began quietly and ordinarily, the way he
> liked and assured himself of. The morning light of
> early autumn rose in the east and filtered through
> the old, cracked windows of the antique shop,
> rattling at the slightest breeze, carrying with it
> smells of dust and wood shavings and varnish.
>
> Every morning for nine years, before the sun
> fully slipped from its covers, Clay had unlocked the
> old shop. The store was tidy and presentable, like a
> perfectly tailored suit, showcasing the uniqueness
> of all the antiques. Everything, as it always did, had
> its place.
>
> This morning he stood in the midst of them,

carefully surveying the room and inventorying what he might need to acquire this week. Some items he found at estate sales. Others, the more unique pieces, George brought his way. Most needed, at the very least, a good buffing, but typically they needed much more. They came to him as trash. But with hard work—tried and true elbow grease—there was rarely anything that couldn't be restored. There was no magic in it, but sometimes when he was finished, it felt otherworldly. A piece would arrive at his doorstep hopeless and pathetic and leave him one day treasured and beautiful.

Wax did wonders. So did sandpaper. And paint.

But the truth was, not everything could be fixed.

It was this early part of the morning that he loved so much, before the busyness of the day began. At the back part of the shop, through the swinging doors, was his little slice of heaven, where the smell of sawdust stirred in him a delight he'd never been able to fully explain to another soul.

Clay set his keys and coffee mug aside, keeping the front lights off because Mrs. Hartnett had a bad habit of dropping by before the crack of dawn if she saw a light on. He knelt beside the small rocker he'd been working on the last several days. An elderly man had dropped it off, hardly saying a word, paying for it in advance even though Clay insisted he didn't need to do that.

"What's your story?" he murmured, his fingers gliding over the now smooth wood. The chair was a hard-bitten thing when it came in, chipped and cracked and neglected, vaguely smelling of smoke. Whenever he worked on an old piece of furniture, or anything else for that matter, he found his mind wandering to possibilities of where it once came from and how it had gotten to where it was now. Most pieces had spent dark days in attics and basements and back rooms that never heard footsteps. Somewhere in their lives, they'd served a good purpose. The lucky ones stayed in the house, but sat invisibly in a corner or by a couch, an annoying place to have to dust, a thorn in the side of someone who wished it could be thrown away, except for the guilt attached because it belonged to a great-grandmother who'd spent her very last pennies to acquire it, or some such story.

Yesterday he'd cut and whittled the rocker's new back slot pieces and today he would stain them. Clay grabbed the sandpaper and walked to the table saw where the slats waited, lined up like soldiers. As he ran the sandpaper across the wood, he could practically hear the creak of the rocker and the laughter of delighted children in another century.

He sighed, rolled up his sleeves, and sanded more quickly. Sometimes he thought *he'd* been born in the wrong century. There was hardly a kid today who would care about sitting in a rocker on the edge of a porch and watching a spring storm blow in. The world that he once thrived in had become a noisy, clangoring, messy place. But here, in the back of the shop, with sawdust spilling through shafts of dusty light, he found his peace.

Rene Gutteridge (aka The Novelist)

POV Comparison (Sample D)
As you can see in the script, this is a visual scene with no dialogue. There is sound and picture. Writer Rik Swartzwelder is painting a very specific image of the character's life. He is isolated, perhaps on purpose. He is passionate about his work. Around him are all the things he's worked on in the back workshop of his antique store.

So as the novelist, I have to approach this scene differently than Rik does. I can't be a camera showing all of this to the reader. This entire scene must be *seen* through the eyes of the character of Clay Walsh. I have to paint this same picture but it must run through his mind. It's not that he just sees the rocker, but *how* does he see the rocker? What does he feel when he sees it?

Because this is the first scene in the script, and also in the book, I have to take the time to establish some of who Clay is. I do this primarily through point of view. How Clay sees this little world he is in—this woodworking shop—tells us a great deal about him. The setting is important, but more important is how Clay sees and interacts with it.

Note several points:

- In the script, Clay's clothing and hair are described. In the book, I don't do this because we're seeing the world through Clay's eyes, and one doesn't normally stop to comment on his or her own hair and outfit. There are ways I could work that in, if it were important to the book here, but it's not, so I left it out.

- Notice all the sounds in the script. In the book, I can work with all five senses: sight, sound, touch, smell and taste.

- Because we're not in Clay's head in the script, we don't get to feel his delight in his work like we can in the book. In the movie, the actor will need to portray this. But in the book, it's up to the writer to bring Clay to life and make him interesting.

As you work with point of view, remember that main difference between the script and the book will be how the scenes are told from the character's eyes. So sink yourself down into the scene (in this case, the workshop), get on your character's level and observe everything from his POV. You are not looking at him through the lens of a camera. His eyes become the lens from which all things are viewed.

The next sample, from *Heart of the Country*, shows a scene with a lot of dialogue. Read the script scene (by John Ward) knowing that I chose Faith as the POV character once I did the novelization.

* * *

SAMPLE E

INT. OLIVIA'S HOUSE — DINING ROOM — LATER

The small table just off the kitchen in the rural farmhouse is a simmering cauldron of passive aggression waiting to boil over. All that is heard is the clanging of silverware on the ceramic plates with the sharper daggers coming from the eyes than used to cut the meat.

> OLIVIA
> Been meaning to ask you
> when you decided to go
> blonde?

Faith looks around the table of brunettes.

> FAITH
> About a year ago.

> OLIVIA
> Saw in the tabloids at the
> grocery store that a bunch
> of celebrities were bleaching
> it now. Guess that's the
> thing…

                          HARDY
          I think it looks nice.

Hardy   spoke   reflexively   and   without
thinking.   He pays the price with a look
from his wife.

                          CALVIN
          I do too, Hardy.

Calvin bails out his son-in-law.

Victoria, the youngest, speaks with the
honesty of a child.

                          VICTORIA
          You look like a princess.

                          FAITH
          Thank you, sweety. That
          makes Auntie Faith feel
          nice.

                          NELL
          She looks like a rock star.

                          FAITH
          Not in this lifetime.

A few looks dart around the table, and
people return to eating.   The ray of
sunshine again replaced by a cloud.   The
sounds of dinner return.

                          CALVIN
          Hardy, I heard you guys got
          in a little hunting yesterday.

Finally, something he wants to talk about.

                          HARDY
          Got a five-point buck.

                    CALVIN
          Did you really? Where abouts?

                    HARDY
          Down in the runs—about a
          quarter mile from Jeffrey's
          crossroads.

                    CALVIN
          They're running down there
          this year?

As Hardy nods, Olivia interjects.

                    OLIVIA
          Hardy tried a new marinade.
          Like it?

                    CALVIN
          Tender.

                    HARDY
          I tried to put in a little
          more lemon juice this time,
          added a teaspoon.

                    CALVIN
          That's a good idea.

As Hardy and Calvin talk deer meat, Olivia
shoots a glance to Faith as she tries to
push the meat out of view on her plate—
you're in my world now, sister.

                    OLIVIA
          So where's Luke?

                    FAITH
          He's in New York.

                    OLIVIA
          Has he ever been down
          here? I can't remember.

                    FAITH
          No. Never been.

                    OLIVIA
          To each his own.

She takes a bite…holding the room.

                    OLIVIA (CONT'D)
          I mean, I know things are
          different up there… I just
          think family's important,
          that's all.

                    FAITH
          And I don't?

Olivia looks up from her plate at the
challenge from her little sister.

Calvin too, pays close attention.

                    OLIVIA
          I don't know, Faith. I
          guess actions speak louder
          than words in my book.

Faith chooses to take her growing
frustration out on her plate of casseroles,
venison, beans, and potato salad. Nothing
looks good. She slides her plate away.

                    OLIVIA (CONT'D)
          Funny how family can be a pain
          and you just think, why
          bother? Then you get fed up
          with your snotty Yankee husband—
          and here you are.

                    CALVIN
          That's enough, Olivia.

                    OLIVIA
          Somebody's gotta say something,
          Daddy. She hasn't been home
          in what…four years?

Faith gets up to leave. Calvin takes her
hand and firmly but lovingly motions for her
to sit.

                    CALVIN
          Now listen—you are sisters.
          We're gonna sit down, and
          we're gonna have Sunday
          dinner. That's it.

Everyone returns to eating with a horrible
tension.

                    HARDY
          Ole number 9 won Darlington
          again.

                    CALVIN
          I saw that. I'll tell you, that's
          the best team in racing.

                    HARDY
          It's not the driver, it's the
          car.

                    CALVIN
          You still gotta get in there
          and press the gas though.

Olivia continues her glare. Faith is
miserable. She looks over to Calvin who
winks at her.

                    * * *

To follow are pages from the novel of *Heart of the Country* from Faith's POV:

"Dinner's served," Olivia called.

"Not eating on the TV trays?" Dad asked as he walked into the dining room. Again, he was kind of pouting like a kid.

"Dad..." Olivia said, in a chiding sort of way. "We have a special guest with us. She deserves more than a TV tray."

The word *guest* stung, but I figured that Olivia already knew that.

We sat down and Dad said grace. When was the last time I'd prayed? At least this kind of prayer. Yeah, I'd thrown up some desperate prayers lately, but nothing calm. Nothing meaningful.

I looked up after the "Amen" to find Olivia watching me. She glanced away as she passed the potatoes.

"Been meaning to ask you when you decided to get your hair bleached that blonde," Olivia said. I tucked my hair behind my ears. "Saw in the tabloids at the grocer that a bunch of celebrity types were bleaching their hair too. Guess that's the thing." She handed me the radishes. "You always looked better in more the dishwater color, I think. Better with your skin."

"Looks real nice, Faith," Hardy said.

That created a perfectly awkward moment, saved only by Nell who said, "I think you look like a princess."

Victoria piped in, "If she's got muscles she could be a pro-wrestler."

Nell glared at her. "She doesn't look like a wrestler, Vic."

"I'm just sayin', she could be one if she wants."

"Girls," Olivia said.

"Okay," Victoria continued, not skipping a

beat, "maybe not a wrestler. I know! A rock star!"

I smiled at her. "Not in this lifetime." But I was kind of dying. I didn't want to be the topic of conversation.

Luckily Dad bailed me out. "Hardy, I heard you guys got in a little hunting yesterday."

"Got a five-point buck."

"Did you really?" Dad set down his fork. "Whereabouts?"

"Down in the runs — about a quarter mile from Jeffrey's crossroads."

"They're running down there this year?"

Hardy nodded and I enjoyed my meal, and the conversation. When I was a kid I hated all the talk about hunting. But now it soothed me, like gentle thunder rolling across the plains.

Olivia sliced her meat, but her eyes looked sharper than the knife. "Hardy tried a new marinade. Like it?" She left my gaze and glanced around the table, I guess so she wouldn't look inappropriate.

But I was sure she wanted to see my expression when I realized I was eating deer meat.

"Tender," Dad said.

"I tried to put a little more lemon juice this time…added a teaspoon."

"That's a good idea."

I nodded in agreement but pushed the meat to the side. Wasn't a big meat eater anyway. And Olivia knew *Bambi* was my favorite movie. Man, she was stooping low.

"So where's Luke?" she asked.

Or maybe lower. I measured my response. "He's in New York."

"Has he ever been down here? I realize he hasn't been to Columbus County, but I meant North Carolina in general."

"No. Never been." It was getting harder to stay

measured. I kept my knife in my hand even though I was just eating the mashed potatoes now.

"To each his own." Olivia shrugged.

I set down my utensils and stared at her.

"No insult intended," she said, slicing her way through her own bull. "I mean, it'd be great if Luke visited. I just think family's important, that's all."

"And I don't?"

Olivia looked at me. Her expression said everything. *This is my turf. You ran away. I wish you'd never returned.* She sat straighter, her eyebrows raised like she was lecturing a child. "I don't know, Faith. I guess actions speak louder than words in my book."

I glanced at Dad. He looked as wounded as the deer we were eating.

"Funny how family can be a pain and you just think, *Why bother?* Then you get fed up with your snotty Yankee husband, and here you are."

"That's enough, Olivia." Dad threw his napkin on the table.

Now Olivia looked wounded. Her eyes swelled with held-back tears. "She hasn't been home in what, almost ten years?"

"Now listen to me. You are sisters. We're gonna sit here and have dinner. And tomorrow we're gonna go to church together. And that's it." Dad picked up his napkin, folded it, and continued eating. Hardy did the same. The girls looked like they'd never seen anything like this before.

"Ole number nine won Richmond again." Hardy had put a gentle hand on Olivia's shoulder. She shrugged it off.

"Saw that, Hardy. I'll tell you, that's the best team in racing."

"It's not the driver. It's the car."

"You still gotta get in there and press the gas though."

The two men went on to talk. Olivia stared at her plate, cutting food she never intended to eat. I did the same. We were as far apart as two people could be. Except for maybe Luke and me. But then again, Luke didn't hate me.

Rene Gutteridge (aka The Novelist)

POV Comparison (Sample E)

As mentioned, in this particular project, I chose the rarely used device of multiple first-person. This means that I write in first-person for each character in whom I invest a POV. Normally in a first person novel, I take one character and I'm in their perspective the entire novel. Multiple first-person allows me to be intimate with all the characters, and because this was a family drama with a lot of good, deep characters, I chose to do it this way. I've never written another novel like this before or since, so that shows you how rarely it's used. It's got to be the right story.

In the book, I am in both Olivia's and Faith's POVs many times. They are both main characters. I am not in Calvin's or Hardy's. So for this scene, I had to choose whether to tell it from Olivia's or Faith's point-of-view. I chose Faith's for several reasons. First, I decided to go into Olivia's POV in the previous chapter, when she is preparing this meal. We see her frustration at her sister being home under these circumstances. It is a chapter and scene I totally made up for the book and is not in the script.

I also thought, since Faith is the one who's being assaulted and insulted, we should be in her head. That makes for a more dramatic scene, as she's processing all of this. In this scene, Faith has the most at stake. That told me her POV would be the most compelling.

So again, I sink myself down into this scene and get into Faith's head. What does she see? *How* does she see it? The deer meat is a perfect example. If this were told through Olivia's, Hardy's or Calvin's POV, the deer meat would barely be mentioned. It's just a way of life for them.

But for Faith, the city girl, it's obviously disturbing. It's the little details that make the difference in how your character sees his or her world and that makes POV special.

If the POV is told by the same narrative voice, with all the characters sounding the same, it's not as powerful. So think like your character, then write him like that.

You'll notice I took out a line that Faith says: "That makes Auntie Faith feel nice." I did that because in a previous chapter, one of the young kids says something about "Aunt Faith" and Olivia remarks that "Aunt" is a title that needs to be earned. Since I'd sort of visited that theme already, I chose to take it out here.

Just like in a screenplay, you'll need to look at the big picture of the novel to see what can stay put and what must leave. Mostly, though, this scene is a good example of the adaptation working seamlessly and staying intact. I added some front-end dialogue, added detail and interior monologue, and finished the scene off with some thoughts from the character, and that was it!

Point of View Exercise
Pick a story and character you're working on. Hold your hand up to your eye like you're filming a movie. Now walk around your house and make a running commentary (out loud) of how your character sees the world.

Next, take a different character and do the same thing. Be cognizant of the differences in how they see the world. One character may look out the window at the snow and feel depressed. The other may be giddy and start counting how many days till Christmas. Do this with as many characters as possible, even secondary characters, to get a feel for how they see the world.

Next we will take a look at structure and plot and give you important questions to ask about them before you do your adaptation.

Chapter Five

STRUCTURE & PLOT

Rene Gutteridge (aka The Novelist)

Key Questions for Structure & Plot

If you are writing the novelization, you will need to evaluate some key questions before starting the process. You will need to analyze the plot of the script and the way the scenes are structured to determine what will be able to remain the same and what will need to be changed. Changes to the structure can include such things as cuts, combining scenes, shifting them around in a different order, or adding new scenes.

Below are some questions you'll want to ask yourself and consider as you're adapting a script. These will help you evaluate the structural or plot changes that you'll want to make, and also help you identify how to accomplish what the script does, but in a different way.

1. **What scenes from the script need to be cut?** Scenes that are in the script only for visual and establishing purposes are not needed in a novel as their own scene. You'll describe places as you enter the scene, when needed, so an "establishing shot" won't be needed. You also won't be able to use scenes where a POV character isn't present. You have the option of trying to get a POV character in there, but if it's

not possible, the scene will have to go. Typically not too many scenes will need to be outright cut from the story. Usually there is a way to work them in.

2. **What scenes need to be added?** This is where you'll be doing most of your work. A typical 90-page script, when adapted as is, turns out to be around 40,000 words in novel form (which works if you are contracted to write a novella). But most full-length novels need to be at least 80,000. The novelist will need to fill in a lot of scenes. This is not as hard as it might seem because unfortunately, screenwriters have to cut a ton of scenes to make their scripts fall into their page count, or for budgetary reasons. As you read the script, you'll be able to tell where scenes could be added to fill in the story. Because movies move fast, scenes that aren't there typically are not missed, but readers are on a slower journey, so you'll want to fill in those scenes.

    You can consider expanding short script scenes into longer novel scenes. In the end, these expansions are like treasure hunts as you delve deeper into the mind of the character, the way actors do to infuse their performances with a rich inner life, beyond the lines they speak. Actors call that subtext. The text (their lines) only explore the tip of the iceberg, but as novelists we get to dive deep and explore so much that is hidden below the surface.

    There's no formula for this. It's more of a gut feeling. It will also depend on your POV choices. Sometimes you have to add scenes to make everything make sense. Typically you're not adding new storylines. You're filling in ones that are already there. You can also add scenes that happen off-screen in the script version, if it will enhance the storytelling.

3. **What scenes need to be lengthened or combined?** When I evaluate a script, I try to identify scenes that, if I can't add to them, can be threaded together. I first look at a scene to see if I can add to the beginning and the end to make it long enough. If that won't work, then I see if I can combine a scene with another one. In fiction, you don't have to have one scene per location. So a scene can start in one city and you can have your character drive to another city and it can be all in one scene. It has to, of course, be written creatively and hold the interest of the reader, but scenes can connect well in novels.

    Movie scripts rely on quickness. Every minute counts. Every minute costs. Because movies are told visually, they often have short scenes, used for a variety of reasons — set ups, flashbacks, crosscuts, the list goes on.

    Shorts scenes in novels are, as a rule, rare. You'll see them every once in awhile, but as I mentioned before, they are there for impact. They're meant to make a statement. Because of how novels are told with interior monologue, a reader can grow weary of short scenes that jump all over the place.

    Combining scenes also comes into play with scenes that are crosscut in scripts. As mentioned before in our discussion of "challenges," a novel can't be "cutting" back and forth between characters. So you can choose how to structure these types of crosscuts. Either pick one POV and tell the whole scene from one point of view, or tell half the scene from one point of view, make a scene break, and tell the other half from another point of view.

Also, short flashback scenes may need to be told in one long scene. Instead of the character "seeing" it in pieces throughout the script, he will need to think about it in bigger chunks in the novel.

4. **Which scenes (or pieces of scenes) need to be in a different order?** This is hard to know off the bat, but you'll begin to identify story timelines that are more difficult to tell in novel format. Multiple flashbacks may need to be put early on in order for the reader to understand the timeline.

   Also, when you're working in multiple points of view, the timeline is extremely important. You may have to reorder scenes to make sure that the series of events you're writing about rolls out correctly per each character's POV of the event. The great thing about timelines in books is that when you change POVs, you can go back in time a little bit. It's not done often and you can't get away with a lot, but it's within your parameters as a novelist to do that.

5. **How should I handle any flashback scenes?** Moments told in flashbacks in a script are often folded into other scenes in a novel or revealed through interior monologue. Flashbacks in film, typically, are used to show what a character is thinking or feeling or to give a slice of backstory. Because you're already in your

characters' heads, in their thoughts and feelings, then a lot of the purposes of flashbacks in film become obsolete in a book. You can easily show what your character is thinking with the interior monologue.

6.   **What backstory necessitates a flashback?** In writing, when we talk about immediate scene, we're talking about a scene that is filmable, to put it in understandable terms to a screenwriter. Sometimes instead of just thinking about something happening, we want the reader to be there, present in it, "watching it happen." Any event that would read well as its own scene, that happened before the story started, can qualify as a flashback. Flashbacks in fiction should be used judiciously. They're more impactful if there are fewer of them.

In *Heart of the Country*, there were flashbacks of an accident involving a deceased character. I chose to write these tiny flashbacks as their own scenes because of the power I felt it brought to the story. In a sense, they are flashbacks in the story because they are out of order with the rest of the timeline. The reader knows this immediately and is able to follow where this belongs in the timeline. But because of the power of this scene, I'm able to use it in this way.

Ask yourself, is this a big enough scene – in a storytelling sense – for it to need its own scene? If so, consider writing it as a flashback. If it's just there for a small purpose, then don't give it its own scene and find another way to get the information in the novel.

7. **For any information that comes out in voice-over, which scenes will those slices of information be added to?** Voice-over is tricky. In scripts it's used to establish character, time, or give information quickly. So you've got to decide the reason it's used in the script and then try to get that into the book, however you feel it best fits. In *Never the Bride*, I felt the voice-over really established Jessie's character, and I had that voice-over in mind when I wrote the opening scene of the book. It especially established the dream she wanted most in life. Beyond just trying to get the "text" in there, I needed to get the purpose in there. Ask yourself what the voice-over is used for and you'll find a good place to incorporate it.

8. **If I have to cut a scene because there is no POV character in the scene, which scene will the information from that cut scene get added to?** This has to be considered on a case-by-case basis. Every decision you make regarding scenes, their order, and whether they stay or go will have a ripple effect. The novelist, as does any writer, must consider how it affects other parts of the story. Understanding the purpose behind the scenes you're working from will help you understand exactly how to put in all the parts.

* * *

Cheryl McKay (aka The Screenwriter)

Plotting in Color
You may have noticed the multi-colored bulletin board on the cover of this book. It includes scene cards from *Never the Bride*. When I first wrote the script, every storyline had its

own color assigned. With a novelization, you'll be doing this work in reverse, just like I do when I get a job adapting a book into a screenplay. And you can use color to help you!

When I adapt a novel, like *The Ultimate Gift*, I make a list of each storyline. For example, this could include the love story, the assignments in Jason's grandfather's will, the sick child, and the dysfunctional family. Each storyline gets assigned its own color. When I read the novel, I use highlighters throughout to color-code key scenes for each storyline. Since I choose a different color for each, coloring up the novel helps me quickly identify scenes that are key to each storyline.

Novelists can do the same with the script. Write a list of storylines, choose a color for each one, and go through the script highlighting each scene (or scene heading) in its own color. Since you will potentially be combining scenes, being able to search out scenes from the same storyline by color will help you.

I make a new binder for every script project. You can create one for each novelization. You can make binder tabs that apply to your project. For example:

- novelization proposal (with synopsis)
- script (color-coded)
- brainstorms
- character breakdowns
- locations / settings
- research
- thematic notes
- meeting notes

Having a binder and a color-coding system just might make the novelization process easier and more organized.

Structuring Chapter Breaks
I have a final piece of advice on structure, before we show you an example. If you are a screenwriter who will be

doing your own novelizations, part of your structure work for the novel will be choosing chapter breaks. If you have ever written a television show, think of chapter breaks like the moment you would cut out of an act and into a commercial break. Think cliffhangers, plot twists, exciting or dramatic moments that will pull in the reader. The goal with chapter breaks is to make it irresistible for the reader to turn the page.

Next, I am going to walk you through a comparison of structure and plot changes on my script-to-novelization of *Song of Springhill.*

* * *

SAMPLE F

To follow are from two different segments from the *Song of Springhill* screenplay.

EXT. SPRINGHILL, NOVA SCOTIA — DAY

INSERT: OCTOBER 1956.

A sign says: WELCOME TO SPRINGHILL. POPULATION 7,802. A clunker of a car passes. There's no wealth, but lots of charm in the hilly town.

> HANNAH (V.O.)
> Springhill is a wildly unpredictable place that also never changes.

EXT. MAIN STREET - DAY

The street is lined with a church, family shops, a bank. Cheerful SENIOR CITIZENS wave at the clunker from a bench with the words "Liars Bench" painted on it.

> HANNAH (V.O.)
> I didn't grow up here. But
> it's the kind of town that
> embraces you, whether you're
> here for a visit or to stay...

A YOUNG GIRL plays hopscotch in front of All
Saints Church.

EXT. POOL HALL - DAY

The clunker pulls up.

> HANNAH (V.O.)
> ...whether you're searching or
> running. Coming here was my
> last hope, one day before
> the Number 4 Mine exploded.

(For this sample, we will jump to a scene
much later into the script. A friendly,
non-date between Hannah and the man who
likes her, Josh.)

EXT. HEATHER'S BEACH — NIGHT

It's a starry night. Hannah walks down the
shoreline. Josh points to a row of cottages
that overlook the water.

> JOSH
> I used to come here every
> summer when my mother was alive.
> We used to rent a cottage right
> up there.

> HANNAH
> Did your mother... did she try
> to stop you from working?

                        JOSH
            We always knew I'd have to work
            in the mines as soon as I was
            seventeen. As you know with
            Abby, compensation when someone
            passes never pays enough.

                        HANNAH
            But you stayed there. Even
            after your mother died.

                        JOSH
            It's the only life I know.

                        HANNAH
            Did your mom ever remarry?

                        JOSH
            No, she and my dad... they
            were like one person. Once he
            was gone, she was only a half.

                        HANNAH
            I never want to be half a person.

                        JOSH
            Is that why it had to be just
            dinner?

                        HANNAH
            It happened to my mother, too.
            I get weary of everyone making
            her out to be this, this hero.
            I think she was a coward.

                        JOSH
            Didn't she choose you over
            herself?

                    HANNAH
          Not because of me. I grew up
          with her sister in Toronto.
          All I heard was the story of
          my mother's great sacrifice.
          But let's be honest. She was
          too sad to live without my
          father. To live without her
          child, too? Of course, she
          sacrificed herself. That's
          what love does. Causes pain
          no one can live with.

When Josh moves to touch Hannah's face, she
shies away.

                    JOSH
          I won't hurt you.

                    HANNAH
          You can't promise me that.

                    JOSH
          Not in the way someone else
          has.

She loses eye contact with him. He raises
her chin back up and kisses her. She allows
him to, then pulls away.

                    HANNAH
          Please, don't do that again.

                    * * *

To follow are pages from Cheryl's novelization of *Song of Springhill*:

October 30, 1956
Hannah peeked out of the guestroom. Rhythmic snores droned from the master bedroom, like they

were in stereo sync. They wouldn't wake for hours. Maybe even noon. But today, she wouldn't be here at noon. Adrenaline surged through her thin frame. Her legs trembled.

This had to work. This was not a time for one of her miscalculations or poor judgment calls. She'd been accused of that a lot lately. Whether it was true or not.

She clutched two suitcases, then took one last look around her room.

So much she was leaving behind. Clothing, shoes, cheap jewelry. Most of it chosen for her anyway. She had packed what mattered; she was sure of it. One last glance at the closet. There was that garment bag. A knowing settled over her, as warm as the midday sun. She would never wear what was inside that bag. It was not coming with her.

Memories flooded as she ducked into the shadowed hallway. She held her breath. Too long, she'd endured the bitter here. Wave upon wave, it had pounded her shores, overwhelming the sweet. Now, with each creak of the floorboards beneath her feet, her spirits lifted.

As she neared the front door, she couldn't bring herself to look into the living room. The shiny, black grand piano she'd dusted every single day before she sat down to play for the past three years would stay here. She'd find a way to buy one of her own someday; she was sure of that. Even if she had to find twenty extra music students to pay for it.

Outside, the gravel crunched beneath her feet. At the car door, the key shook in her hand. It clattered against every part of the metal except the hole. She used her other hand to steady it, till it finally went in.

Gently, she put the suitcases into the backseat, the same two she'd used since she was a teenager.

All she'd keep of her life's belongings fit inside a pair of cubes. But she had what she needed, including the journal.

His journal.

The only treasure she had of his, tucked inside the pocket of one of the suitcases. All of it, in her daddy's handwriting. She'd read it so many times that she had most of his entries—his prayers—memorized.

A thud resounded. Hannah whipped around toward the cottage. Had someone heard her? She didn't spot anyone, and the front door remained closed.

It was time to test her 1947 blue Studebaker Champion, see if she still had enough champ left in her to make the trip. The Champ was hardly new when Hannah bought her. Winters and salt laden roads had eaten away parts of the frame since, yet she had a hum to her—some may call it a rattle—that soothed Hannah like the lullaby her mama used to sing. It was familiar and always there. But not a sound she wanted lighting up the neighborhood when trying to escape unnoticed. The Champ was her first big possession, paid for with what little money she'd managed to tuck away from those music lessons she'd given.

Those kiddos were the only people she'd miss from this city. The way Eli cheered when he finally got the C sharp minor chord right on the guitar. Or the way Joy beamed when her right hand could play a different rhythm than her left on the piano. Now, that was a special talent. Not everyone had it. Hannah knew well how to blaze across the keys in different rhythms; it came so naturally to her. But the same did not characterize her life; it always seemed out of sync, especially with her desires.

An ache knotted Hannah's throat. She couldn't say goodbye to those kids. She'd had to keep far too many secrets these days. Telling them about this—planning for this exact moment—she couldn't do it.

Headlights turned the street corner, startling her. She ducked down behind the car in the driveway, hoping whichever neighbor was coming home at this hour didn't see her. The vehicle passed with a whir. She waited a couple more seconds, released her breath, then slid onto the driver's seat.

She steeled herself against tossing up a prayer as she pulled the door closed. No, it wasn't needed; this was up to her alone. She could do this. And she wasn't sure anyone would listen anyway. She had prayed enough for intervention in the past.

That her mother wouldn't die, for starters.

But it would be fine. All she had to do now was push on that gas and fix her eyes on her destination.

Her neck throbbed. As she glanced in the rearview, the purple bruises were still visible. Why didn't she grab her collared sweater? Well, maybe because she hated that dark pink and white garment. It made her look like a wrapped up piece of ribbon candy.

And this would be the last time someone would leave a mark.

Hannah turned the key in the ignition. The Champ sparked to life. Just like that engine, she had the power within her to run, the power to not be a victim any longer. How had she forgotten that for the past three years? It was all a blur. But with the Champ's racket, it was time to get out of here. She pressed on the gas, knowing she'd never see that little yellow cottage again. An unfamiliar feeling, the corners of her mouth turned up.

Her stomach fluttered; she'd waited her entire life. Now, it was time to return to the place her father used to call *home* until twenty-seven years ago.

Until his death, a smattering of hours before

her birth.
   A place called *Springhill.*

Cheryl McKay (aka The Screenwriter)

Structure and Plot Comparison (Sample F)
This is an example of a structure change (adding a sequence that doesn't exist in the script) and a plot change (changing the character's backstory).

In the script version, the first time we see Hannah is her arrival into Springhill. That point in the book comes right after the segment I shared here. In the novel, I wanted to take a little time up-front to plant some seeds about Hannah and what she was escaping from. I saved the details for much later into the script (peppered throughout other scenes), but I felt like I had to establish there were some issues early on and hint at them. I faced the challenge that in the script, Hannah is rather secretive about her past. But when you write a novel and you're inside the character's head, you can't just hide all those secrets. She's not keeping them from herself. Not using her as a POV character was not an option. So I used the opening to establish she had secrets, even though I don't put all the detail in there just yet. Remember, when it comes to secrets: hint. When it comes to details, dot rather than dump. Just add enough at a time to keep the reader engaged.

I also wanted a way to establish her backstory with her family, her mother, and her ties to Springhill before her arrival. The second script scene shows what a key piece of backstory *used to be* regarding my lead character, Hannah, and her mother: that her mother died in childbirth. You probably noticed from the novelization pages that I changed that backstory for the novel.

When I started writing the opening sequence to establish Hannah, once I was inside her head, I felt a little handicapped in being able to explore her family history if her mother wasn't there to share things with her. I knew I wanted her mother to have passed on at the story's opening when she travels to Springhill. Yet, I felt like it bought me more to have Hannah's history change: that she had her mother for a while when she was younger.

In the novel segment I shared, Hannah mentions how she prayed for her mother to not die. Obviously, this wasn't the childbirth death of the script, and she was old enough to remember when it happened. What exactly happened is included later into the novel when she's finally talking to someone about her history. But none of that is needed in the script.

Having her mother alive for a time helped me several times throughout the novel when there were facts I needed Hannah to know about her father, especially as revealed through her interior monologue. A lot of those were details I didn't need in the script but felt they helped the novel version. I also had the chance to include a few memories.

None of these changes take the novel far away from the script, but they made the novel easier to write and the character and history easier to set up.

You will be able to make the same types of choices in your novelizations, to make sure they best serve the novel. As Rene has stressed, a novel must stand on its own. And it's your job to make sure it does! And sometimes that means plot and structure changes.

Next up is interior monologue, all those interior thoughts that novelists get to play with, to dig deep into the inner life of characters.

Chapter Six

INTERIOR MONOLOGUE

Cheryl McKay (aka The Screenwriter)

What is Interior Monologue? Is it already in the script?
Thoughts, private gripes, concerns, dreams, hopes, fears, secrets unspoken, private jokes. Will you find these in a screenplay? While novelists can let you peek inside their characters' minds, screenwriters cannot. If they try to include an internal thought in a line of description or in a parenthetical above the dialogue, what are they told? "Only write what you see and hear on the page!" "We can't read your character's mind so cut that out of your script!"

Screenwriters have to live with opposite writing rules from novelists. They get nailed for giving information about a character's thought life. Normally, the only line of description where they are given latitude is when introducing a character for the first time. They can include a description we don't necessarily see or hear on screen. Screenwriters are given one or two sentences of grace to convey attitude, personality, and a slice of who the character is to guide the script reader in how to imagine a character. But otherwise—for the rest of the script—forget it! They must stick exclusively to two arenas: *what the camera sees and the microphone picks up.* (Screenwriters: doesn't that make you all want to become novelists?)

Even when a screenwriter puts a parenthetical right before the dialogue to guide the actor in how to say the line—like labeling it sarcastic or joking—that's frowned on. That doesn't stop it from happening, though. Apparently, parentheticals annoy actors. (They're taught in acting classes to cross them out!) No one cares that it annoys the screenwriter when the actor misses the point of that dialogue. While it's the director's job to make sure actors portray the lines correctly, there's no guarantee a director will interpret a writer's line the way the writer intended. Most directors don't talk to screenwriters about scripts before they're shot; they want to create their own interpretations of stories. So if screenwriters want to write for that world, they must play by the rules and stick to writing what's seen and heard.

What's seen and heard.

However, this is where having a script novelized opens up a different world. One of the biggest gems of novel writing is expanding the thought life of the character(s). While movies depend on the actors and director to bring the inner life of the characters to the big screen, it's readers who get to cast whom they picture and how they hear the lines spoken. Novel readers may not have the benefit of actors showing them how they feel, but the readers' imaginations can spark to life, thanks to the talent of the novelist.

Keep this in mind: if the screenwriter is not novelizing the script, it helps if there is a good working relationship between the two writers. If a novelist is willing to show chapters along the way, especially early on, it can help to have the screenwriter's eye to catch inconsistencies. For example, if a novelist begins to craft interior monologue the screenwriter knows won't work for what's coming later in the script—or even a sequel in the works—those problems can be addressed before the novelist writes herself into a corner. That screenwriter is going to know the details of the story more intimately than the novelist will. (A novelist may have read the script a handful of times before diving in, but that screenwriter has probably combed through her draft twenty or more times!)

As a screenwriter, watching the expansion of the interior monologue of my characters has been one of the most fascinating aspects of working with a novelist. Naturally, writing internal thoughts gives the novelist a dynamic tool to expand length. They can take what the screenwriter provided, and blow it up on the page.

In a film scene, a dialogue exchange may take just a few moments because the lines are spoken back and forth. Yet a novelist can pause and let the reader know what one character thinks about what the other just said. When penning a script, I may know what my characters think even if it's not spelled out on that white page in Courier New 12 point. The hope is the expressions on the actors' faces will allow the audience to fill in those blanks. But getting to see this expansion — up close and personal in the novelizations of my scripts — has been so much fun! This device can bring a scene in a book to life. A ten second piece of dialogue in a script can easily turn into three pages of story using interior monologue.

So how do we do it?

* * *

Rene Gutteridge (aka The Novelist)

Do's and Don'ts of Interior Monologue
Think about the most narcissistic person you know. It's all about me, me, me, right? Many novels suffer the same plight — they become narcissistic in their pursuit to reveal their characters' thoughts. It's particularly true for first-person POV but don't think third person is off the hook either. Both rely on interior monologue to get through a story. So, what is interior monologue and why do we need to be so careful using it?

Interior monologue is the thoughts of your characters as it pertains to the story. It consists of the inwardly spoken thought-life, a sensory response to what they encounter. It is one of the big distinctions between film and books, and it is why books seem to connect more deeply to readers. We feel like we've gotten to know characters more when we are able to know their thoughts. It's like we're part of the inside circle.

But the problem is this: if you had to hear my thoughts all day long about every single thing, you'd jump off a cliff from sheer boredom or vast confusion. The truth is that people's thoughts are not, in general, that interesting for long periods of time, and they're more jumbled than coherent. So storytelling is an illusion. Alfred Hitchcock said it best when he equated a good story to life, minus all the dull parts.

Interior monologue follows the same rule: it is thoughts, with all the dull, weird, or incoherent parts taken out. I always think of the best interior monologue as worthy of eavesdropping. We only eavesdrop on conversations that catch our interest.

The trap for most new writers is that they have too much interior monologue and what they have is too boring. Interior monologue should not be confused with stream-of-consciousness. You know those writing assignments where you were told to journal everything that came to mind? Don't do that here. Instead of creating cliffhangers, you'll create cliff jumpers.

As badly as it can turn out, interior monologue is a lot of fun to write. In the case of novelizations, it's one part of our craft that will set the novel apart from the script. While a script depends on visual cues to alert the audience to what an actor might be thinking, a novel can dive right in and show it by painting pictures with words.

So before I give you some tips on how to do it, let me tell you how *not* to do it. Here are three DON'Ts that you'll want to keep in mind while writing:

1. **Don't make the mistake of believing that interior monologue is simply your character's thoughts.** It's way more than her thoughts. *It's how your character <u>sees</u> the world.* If she is a

painfully shy young woman, then she must see the world through those painfully shy eyes. If she is bold and sarcastic with a hint of filter, then what comes out of her mouth doesn't begin to touch what pops into her brain. If your character is a child, then she will think about a car accident much differently than an adult would.

2. **Don't make the mistake of halting the story to show interior monologue.** Interior monologue must always carry a story forward, so it is used in much of the same way other devices are — it must present conflict and rise of action and inner turmoil. It becomes stagnant when it serves only one purpose: to let you know what the character is thinking. I always tell writers to make each writing device accomplish more than one task. Dialogue can't just be what characters say. It must stir trouble or create a hook or present a cliffhanger or reveal secret information. Dialogue for the sake of dialogue is sludge to read. The same is true for interior monologue. Your character self-talking her way out of a corner isn't going to read interestingly unless her thoughts create conflict, add mystery, propel the plot forward, reveal something about her, or do something else that proves worthwhile in engaging the reader.

3. **Don't forget interior monologue is an illusion.** It is not what she is thinking; it is what the story requires her to think. Remember Hitchcock's rule, but also remember the rule of eavesdropping. Think about sitting at your favorite coffee shop. What conversations grab your interest? What words arrest your attention? The reader believes he or she is

reading the characters' thoughts, but the reality is that you're using another device to pull the reader deeper into the story and the character.

Now, let's look at some DOs and HOW TOs.

1. **Do be mindful of 'less is more.'** Even in first-person, you can't tell an entire story by thoughts. Interior monologue is a tool like all the other tools you have to tell a great story. Use it sparingly, judiciously, and purposefully. A page of streaming thoughts is less impactful than a single thought set to a single line.

2. **Remember that interior monologue is essentially 'telling.'** If you've read much about novel writing, you know a golden rule is 'show don't tell.' While you can't 'show' your whole story, novel writing is the craft of picking and choosing when to show a scene using action and description, and when to just tell it, for time's sake or to get the story moving. Here are some examples of telling:

> John was nervous.
> John thought, *I feel so nervous.*
> John said, "I'm nervous."

As you can see, even though we're working with different tools in our tool box, these all boil down to telling the reader what is happening. In these examples, you can clearly see that interior monologue is telling. There are instances when it can shift into showing, but mostly it's telling. To show, we might write something like:

> John's hands shook enough that he didn't dare try to pick up his coffee mug and

take a sip. Instead, he just stuck his hands in his pockets and picked at the lint.

Attempt to balance out your showing and telling. Knowing how much of each you're using will help you decide when and where to show or tell.

3. **Do allow interior monologue to do the heavy lifting.** Your character's thoughts reveal a lot and they should. If you knew what I was thinking, you'd have an entirely different outlook about me than you do now. Think about it: why are diaries so secretive? Why do we put them under lock and key? Because they reveal way more than we are comfortable sharing with the world. Remember this discomfort when you're writing. Their thoughts should be as raw as if they drained their blood straight onto the page.

And here's a final tip. Interior monologue relies on interesting characters. So, when taking a character from a script, you've got to be able to read between the lines, plucking him off the page and making him well-rounded and three-dimensional. Where an actor might interpret his character with facial expressions and emphasis on certain words or turns of phrase in his dialogue, the novelist can interpret the character even more deeply—inside his thoughts.

Characters are more interesting when what they're thinking is exactly the opposite of what they're saying out loud. For example, bold inside, wet noodle on the outside. Thoughts, in a way, betray the character. He wants the world to think of him as one way, but the reader gets to know him in another. Readers get the privilege of knowing him in a way nobody else does. You, as the writer, must learn how your character speaks to himself. You must know him that well.

When you read a script, you must look at what is happening in the physical and then go inside the mental. You must look at the outward dialogue and then create another world of inner dialogue. (Like we mentioned in the chapter on POV, this is called subtext.)

Once you decide what your character thinks of life and how he speaks to himself, then you've created your character's voice. That is what will make him distinguishable, inside and out.

To illustrate interior monologue, Cheryl will walk you through a sample from her project, *The Walk*.

* * *

SAMPLE G

To follow are the opening three pages of Cheryl's screenplay for *The Walk,* a pilot episode for a TV series.

EXT. CHURCH - DAY — ESTABLISHING

Dark clouds hover above, aching to rain.

          PASTOR (O.S.)
      "To everything there is a
      season, and a time to every
      purpose under the heaven."

INT. CHURCH — DAY

A funeral is underway. A modest-sized family, young and old, and friends pepper the quaint sanctuary. There's no casket.

Just an easel, which holds a framed photo of a striking woman who was too young to die: ALEXIS "LEXIE" WELLS, 30. The PASTOR, 40's, struggles with the words.

> PASTOR
> "A time to weep, and a time
> to laugh. A time to mourn,
> and a time to dance."

ANNA WELLS, mid-50's, stares at her daughter's photo. Lexie's father, DAVIS WELLS, late 50's, is just as numb.

> PASTOR (CONT'D)
> The Word of God also says
> there's "a time to be born,
> and a time to die."

JAYCIE DAYTON, 7, kicks the pew in front of her. Her mother, HEATHER DAYTON, late 20's, nudges the restless child. Two uniformed Sal's Diner employees sit behind them: SAL, 70's, and IRIS, 50's. Iris silently cries.

> PASTOR (CONT'D)
> That part is always hard
> to understand... when someone
> dies so young. Especially
> the way Alexis--

From the back of the sanctuary: LEXIE WELLS, 30, barges in. She looks just like her photo.

Everyone turns around. They stare at her blankly, not betraying even a hint of recognition. Lexie glances from one face to the next. They turn back to face the pastor. She quickly slips into a back pew.

> PASTOR (CONT'D)
> The way Lexie died...

NICK BRYSON, 30, stunningly handsome, slips in the door so quietly, the guests don't notice. Only the Pastor sees him.

                PASTOR (CONT'D)
       I know it will be a while
       before many of you will find
       peace.

Nick joins Lexie on the back pew. She
ignores him.

                PASTOR (CONT'D)
       I hope you can lean on
       each other--

A BEEPER goes off. Lexie's. Again, disturbed
guests turn around. Lexie pulls out a hand-
held computer device labeled "VELIOGRAPH"
and silences the intruding sound.

Words on the Veliograph crawl: LEAVE THERE
NOW. MICHAEL.

Lexie glances at Sal and speaks quietly to
Nick.

                LEXIE
       What is Sal doing here? He
       could barely tolerate me.

                NICK
       What's not to tolerate?

Lexie rolls her eyes at Nick.

INT. CHURCH FOYER - DAY

Davis shakes guests' hands as they head out.
Anna stands nearby, emotionless.

Lexie and Nick stand in the hallway's
opening to the foyer.

Nick spots the bulletin board, announcing
social events, Bible studies. One poster

says: "MISSING: PROFESSOR NICK BRYSON" with a photo... It's Nick's face. He grabs it.

> NICK
> I hate this picture.

Jaycie, Heather, and her husband, BEN DAYTON, late 20's, walk up to Anna and Davis.

> JAYCIE
> I keep imagining Aunt Lexie
> walking in the door. Is
> that freaky, Grandma?

And Lexie does walk in... to the foyer, staring at Jaycie. Nick steps up behind Lexie and grabs her arm, stopping her.

> HEATHER
> (off Anna's silence)
> Mom. Answer her.

Davis puts his arm around Jaycie.

> DAVIS
> I do that too, Sweetie.

Heather glares at Anna. Ben turns to Jaycie.

> BEN
> And we can always talk about
> the fun times we had with Lexie.

> JAYCIE
> Like when she taught me to
> dance the "kooky racha"?

> HEATHER
> (eyeing Jaycie and Anna)
> Lexie isn't coming back,
> Jaycie. You do understand
> that, right?

Lexie tries to head their direction again, but Nick won't let go of her.

> NICK
> Think of them.

> LEXIE
> I am. How would you feel if
> your family looked at you
> like you're nobody?

> NICK
> To them, that's who you are

Lexie's eyes lock with Anna's. But the recognition isn't there.

> NICK (CONT'D)
> Nobody.

* * *

To follow is the opening scene of *The Walk* in novel form, which is a work-in-progress, to be published as Flip Flop Fiction, a series by Cheryl McKay. There are approximately 12 novel pages adapted from this three-paged sequence of the script. Here, we will share what equals approximately 7 novel pages written in first person, Lexie's POV.

Have you ever wondered what it would be like to show up at your own funeral?

Yeah, not something I imagined happening to me either.

I know he's watching me right now. I'm not allowed to be here, but I really don't care. The list of rules I have to follow are so long: what's the big deal, breaking just one of them? I still have some degree of free will left.

I mean, seriously, would you miss this? I gotta see who showed up to pay their respects. Or more importantly, who didn't. Yeah, that can be telling.

There's got to be some way to see without actually going inside.

I spot a plastic pail near the church's maintenance shed. I'm light enough that it just might hold me. Might. I'm not known for my strong sense of balance.

I grab the pail, try to ignore that it's spattered in mud, march over to a window of the sanctuary and turn it upside down. I'm sure glad I didn't wear stilettoes today.

Okay, confession time. I will never be a model. Never be able to walk with a book on my head for more than two seconds, or in five-inch pumps with a heel the circumference of a pencil. If I try, I fall flat on my butt or face depending on which way the pendulum swings. There, I said it.

Wow, could this place use a paint job. Abundant Life Church needs a makeover and a renewed sense of living up to its name. The grey used to be white; the paint historically covered all the wood. I can't remember how long ago because, well, I haven't exactly been showing up here lately. But when I first started going here, it was definitely clean white.

As I peek through the window, I hear the pastor droning on with a stereotypical verse, one that many families hear during funerals. I think he even preached this one at my grandmother's service twenty years ago.

"To everything there is a season, and a time to every purpose under the heaven."

Yeah, there is a purpose in this, believe it or

not. Actually even a good one. It's just no one in my family is allowed to know what that is. Even if I tried to tell them, they wouldn't believe me. Heck, I wouldn't believe me either.

I still don't quite believe it, and I'm me. I don't make a habit of lying to myself. Most of the time.

A raindrop hits my nose as I crane my neck to see who else is here for the festivities. I should not be surprised it would drizzle on a day like today. Hey, at least it's not my wedding.

I've never had one of those; I wonder if I'll get out of this mess in time to still have one.

Funerals, weddings. They're so similar, aren't they? Food, fellowship. They bring the same family together who ignores each other the rest of the year. "Oh, we must see each other more often," everyone feigns. But do they make the effort?

I wonder if she even cares that I'm gone.

My mother's life…it must be easier now. She has less to be dissatisfied with in life. She looks stoic sitting there, staring at the pastor. She's probably critiquing his sermon inside her head, not realizing, so far, it's all written by Someone else…Someone she ought not critique. I wonder if she's even dripped a tear. She's not big on shedding them, but she sure doesn't mind causing them.

"A time to weep, and a time to laugh. A time to mourn, and a time to dance." The pastor curls the corner of his Bible between his thumb and index finger. That Bible sure looks like it's had a few decades of use.

I spot my seven-year-old niece, Jaycie, sitting next to my sister, Heather. Normally, she's laughing 24-7 minus the occasional nap, but not today. I think she's probably my favorite person on God's green earth. She tends to busy herself making kooky noises that should not be emitted in public. It's odd to see her so subdued. I'd do anything to get rid of that solemn look. If Jaycie doesn't stop biting the bottom corner of her lip, she'll need more than gloss to heal it. And I'm not really in a position for her to steal my Chapstick, like usual.

My father. He's the one I worry about most. Can his heart take this kind of stress? I'm sure my mother will find a way to blame me for that too, even if I'm not here.

Suddenly, I'm filled with this urge to reach out to them, to explain. How can I let them go on, believing what they think? It's so wrong.

I practically fall off the pail and race for the back door of the church. It's like running through mud. You know how you feel when you're trapped in a bad dream and even if you're moving, you don't seem to make any progress?

Except this isn't a dream. It's real. Though my reality is very different than you would think.

Finally, I prevail and barge into the sanctuary.

Okay, I'll admit; it's not the smoothest entrance. Actually, it's loud. Yet bonus: I don't fall flat on my face because I'm minus stilettoes. New Balance is my Old Faithful. This is not exactly how one should enter a quiet, somber occasion, but I've never been conventional.

Maybe that's how I got into this mess.

Suddenly, they're all staring at me. And I mean *all of them*. My mother, father, sister, niece, brother-in-law. Wait a minute. My boss from the diner? Sal showed up? He always hated me. Okay, maybe hate is a strong verb; he tolerated me. And there's Iris. My co-worker. She loved me. Always. Unconditionally. More than once I daydreamed about her being my real mother. You should hear the "lost at birth" scenarios I'd come up with. She--

Wait a minute. *That's* the picture they decided to use? I know there was no need for a casket at this particular shindig. A picture is the next best representation—for a substitute viewing that is—but seriously?

I stare at the 10 by 13, framed-in-fake-gold photo they blew up for this clambake. I have to be ten years younger. What was I…eighteen? Twenty? That's the only one they could dig up?

The glare-down continues for my noisy disturbance, but then they all turn back around and refocus on the pastor. They act like I'm not even here. Well, they know I'm here. I'm not invisible, but apparently they see no reason to talk to me.

I quietly take my seat. Yes, I have it in me to not make a splash. I just don't always put that gift into practice.

"The Word of God also says there's a time to be born, and a time to die."

Yup. Cue the violin. Except they didn't hire a girl with a Stradivarius. I only know what a Strad is because my best friend, Lulu, in high school played one. She got much better grades than me. She's one of those noticeably absent today; she probably doesn't even know this is going on. We stopped talking about eight years ago when she was a prodigy and I was a dropout.

I decide to listen to what the pastor has to say about me. "That part is always hard to understand, when someone dies so young. Especially the way Alexis did."

Alexis. I don't know if I can begin to describe how strange it is to hear the pastor say my name and "dies" as if it happened. It seems so formal. So final. He says it like I'm not in the room.

Suddenly, Nick slides next to me on the pew. No one turns around, but he's got that stealth thing mastered. I didn't even hear him slip in the back door. Only the pastor seems to notice the new attendee to my *alleged* graduation from earth. Yes, I do mean alleged.

Nick. What can I say about Nick? I got him into this, too. Well, sort of. He's not the worst companion I could have chosen for this journey. If only I could forget our history and how attractive he can be, then maybe I could focus on the mission at hand. Maybe then, I could fix this and get us out of this. Because if I am truly honest with myself: this is my fault. If I weren't honest, Nick would remind me.

"Lexie, what are you doing here?" he whispers.

"Could you have stayed away? I mean, if that were your picture up there?"

The pastor continues his sermon: "I know it will be a while before many of you will find peace. I hope you can lean on each other."

Suddenly, the device fastened to my belt sounds an obnoxious beep. This device—it's called a Veliograph. You probably won't find one available at stores. Trust me, if one ever lands in your hands, it means you're in just as much of a pickle as I am.

I've always liked pickles. Especially on salads, and I always order the extra pickles on the Chick-Fil-A Original.

Sorry, did I also mention I'm A.D.D.?

I can't silence the beeping noise fast enough and again, I face those stares.

I read the words: GET OUT OF THERE NOW.

I know who they're from: Michael. He likes to tell us what to do. I've always been known for my defiance. So why would I be any different on this journey?

I didn't ask him to choose me.

Neither did Nick.

* * *

Cheryl McKay (aka The Screenwriter)

Interior Monologue Comparison (Sample G)

To adapt my pilot for a TV series into a novel series, I chose first person POV for my two leads, Lexie and Nick. This opening chapter starts with Lexie's voice. This example also shows how much you can get to know a character by knowing their internal thoughts. It's important to capture the voice of the character so her interior monologue matches the voice of her dialogue.

For me as a screenwriter, doing this expansion was a blast. Lexie is a funny, somewhat sarcastic character. So getting to explore her voice, dive inside her mind, and know her internal thoughts was such fun.

I was able to introduce a lot more backstory by letting you inside her mind. I give hints about the challenges with her mother, how she feels about various members of her family and scratch the surface of introducing Nick. So much of this information is not in the opening script pages but peppered throughout the script instead.

Interior Monologue is my favorite tool novelists have that screenwriters don't: access to these private thoughts. You can open a scene and breathe into it for a while, not rushing through like you would in a script.

Naturally, it's an intriguing situation about why a girl would show up for her own funeral. (And more importantly why no one recognizes her, even though she looks like her own photo.) I don't answer all of those questions up front. The scene serves the same purpose in the script and the novel. However, you walk away from the novel version knowing a lot more or sensing some hints about more story to come that doesn't show up in the script until later.

Interior Monologue Exercise

Now, let's have you put interior monologue into practice with the following exercise. Adapt the following generic scene into novel prose. Choose your POV character and practice filling in what the character thinks about the words spoken by the other character. Even though the dialogue is purposely generic, writing the interior monologue will allow you to reveal what the scene is about and who the characters are to each other. (In acting classes, these are "open scenes" where the actors try to play the subtext of the scene while the audience guesses what the scene is about. In novel form, you get to show us by what you describe.)

> CHARACTER A: Are you going to show up?
> CHARACTER B: I'm thinking about it.
> CHARACTER A: What do you plan to do when you get there?
> CHARACTER B: I'll figure it out when I get there.
> CHARACTER A: Are you hiding something from me?
> CHARACTER B: Of course not. What makes you think that?
> CHARACTER A: Nothing.

* * *

Now that you've practiced your hand at writing interior monologue, let's talk about how to add backstory in the next chapter.

Chapter Seven

BACKSTORY

Cheryl McKay (aka The Screenwriter)

Backstory in Scripts vs. Books
After interior monologue, backstory is one of the other big areas of change from script to novel format. It's one of the most enjoyable tools an author has for expansion. Because screenwriters are limited to writing what's seen and heard in scripts, it can be tough to get backstory told. Flashbacks are sometimes considered a lazy cheat, and yet a novelist can slip into a memory (through interior monologue) with no problem, provided it moves the story forward.

If a character speaks to a friend or family member about a piece of history she already knows, it will come across as expositional. It will sound like a conversation that is only in there so the writer can catch the audience up on the past.

Imagine this scene:

> *Son: Right after I was born, my father left me.*
> *Mom: Yes, Son, it was very sad.*

Silly, right? Characters don't tell others historical pieces of information they already know. It's much harder to get that backstory out in a natural way in a screenplay, when you can't be inside the thoughts of a character. We don't have time for it, it's not interesting, and it sounds like the writer hounding you with information. Screenwriters can try to hide backstory with humor or conflict, so it feels more organic to the story.

For example, you could write the conversation between the mother and son like this:

> *Mom: Where are you going?*
> *Son: To find my father.*
> *Mom: If he didn't want you when you were born,*
> *what makes you think he wants you now?*

The same information is revealed, but the character isn't purposefully telling the other something he or she already knows. Instead, the backstory is hidden in conflict through a scene with a current action (the son about to leave).

Novelists can use either the dialogue to reveal the backstory, veiling it in the same way, or they can climb into the minds of their POV characters. When a novelist supplies backstory, it allows a reader to get to know that character deeper, often quicker than he would in watching a film. While it's still important to "show don't tell" like in a script, novelists have more latitude to dig into the past. Your novelist may get to know more about your characters' lives and pasts than you may have explored writing the script, since what they come up with can land on the page for all to read. As screenwriters, a lot of our backstory work is "behind-the-scenes."

* * *

Rene Gutteridge (aka The Novelist)

Expanding Backstory
You must know your main character's backstory so you can tell his current story. It's not that you will need all of his backstory, but it will be helpful in the immediate scenes to explain why he acts, for example, shy, fearful, or prejudiced. Why is he obsessing over whether his tie is

straight? In his thoughts, it could be a memory of his mother, who always straightened his tie before they left for church. It's introspection at its finest.

When I'm reading a script, I look for signals in the screenplay to find backstory worth expanding. It may be in just one line of dialogue or in a character's glance at a photograph or a reaction to something a character says or the mention of a person from the past. I have to look at the subtext of the dialogue, to see if there are nuggets I can mine out for more drama.

The key to writing good backstory is that it doesn't stop the story. It always propels the story forward.

Here are a few tips about backstory:

- POV characters will always need backstory. I rank my POV characters. Not all are created equal, so you need to list who the main characters are and how their stories impact others around them. The character with the most "screen time" will require the most backstory because that is the character the reader will want to know the most about.

- Resist the urge to tell all the backstory at once. Think about it like dating. On the first date, you don't want to dump your entire past out on the person. Sprinkle the backstory as the reader needs to know it. I like to use backstory as planted "hooks" throughout the story, teasing the reader to turn the page to learn more.

- If you have access to the screenwriter, you might run some of the backstory, at least the crucial points, by her before you get attached to it. Sometimes you can write yourself into a corner if you're not thinking ahead to the rest of the story. The screenwriter knows her script well and can let you know if the backstory conflicts in any way. Also, if there is a sequel to come, make sure your backstory lines up.

* * *

SAMPLE H

To follow is a script page from Cheryl's script, *Ask Riley*. This is one of our works-in-progress.

INT. L.A. TRIBUNE - CURTIS'S OFFICE — DAY

CURTIS MACY, early 40s, mesmerizing good looks, yet professional. Intimidating. A small, framed photo of his WIFE rests on his desk, and he wears a wedding band. His name placard has a title: EDITOR-IN-CHIEF.

The paper's owner, MR. QUACKENBUSH, 60s, a large, barrel-chested man towers over Curtis's desk.

              MR. QUACKENBUSH
You hired her. You get to
fire her.

              CURTIS
Riley has a following.

              MR. QUACKENBUSH
They're turning on her.
Her latest article, *Life is
Like the Movies*... in today's
cynical world, nobody
believes that tripe. We got
emails clogging the mainframe
complaining about it.
We need a new column in
there, something fresh that
sells.

Miranda, the nemesis, listens from outside the door.

>   CURTIS
>   Next week, I'm getting Riley
>   on a national radio call-in
>   show for Valentine's Day
>   week. Maybe that will open
>   up syndication ops.

>   MR. QUACKENBUSH
>   You have 'til the end of next
>   week to prove to me she's
>   worth keeping.

The owner slips out of the office, practically bowling over Miranda on his way out. He ignores her. Miranda steps in Curtis's doorway:

>   MIRANDA
>   Mr. Macy...

>   CURTIS
>   Miranda, where's my storm
>   water run-off article?

Curtis dials a number on the phone.

>   MIRANDA
>   It's coming. I was thinking.
>   Give me a stab at a new--

>   CURTIS
>   Can it wait? I've got something
>   I need to take care of.
>   (on phone)
>   Yes, this is Curtis Macy from
>   the L.A. Tribune. I need to
>   speak with your station manager.
>   I'm following up about booking
>   the Ask Riley columnist.

To follow is the opening of Chapter Two of *Ask Riley,* the novel version:

> From the fourth floor of his windowed, corner-office, Curtis Macy rested uneasily in the leather chair that had been reupholstered five times. Every little creak or groan or squeak that came from it was another reminder of the weighty history the chair brought to every desk by which it sat. The man who occupied its seat was to carry on visions and dreams and consciences of men long dead and gone. Men whose blood Curtis carried in his veins.
>
> His great grandfather, John Levi Macy, helped the three founders of the *Chicago Daily* launch their first edition in 1867. From there, after the *Daily* acquired and absorbed three other Chicago publications, he rallied the new editors towards using the paper to support and push the Abolitionists agenda.
>
> His grandfather, Haddock Macy, worked at the *Chicago Daily* from the ages of ten to forty, learning everything he needed to know about newspaper publishing. He then moved his family to Los Angeles, California, in hopes of going into politics. When a run for the senate failed, he started his own small publication to support his political views. The *California Tribune* was launched in May of 1942. But the task had taken its toll and his grandfather died at his desk of a heart attack in 1943, the day before Christmas, at the age of 45. They found him face down on the early edition.
>
> Curtis's father, Barrett Macy, the only boy born to Haddock, was just a baby when his father died, but the newspaper was managed by Barrett's uncle until he was old enough to take over as managing editor. Twenty years into his father's newspaper career, the newspaper was sold out of desperation to C & A Media Group, and became the *L.A.*

Chronicle in 1979 before it died a slow death in 1981 at the hands of an erroneous report on a senator's affair. His father never worked for another paper and was unemployed until his death in 1986.

So even though he sat in the same chair as the men before him, and worked in the same field as well, the blood in his veins meant nothing to his current employer of three years, *The L.A. Tribune,* or its owner, Mr. Leavenworth, who was presently rounding the corner and blowing into Curtis's office like a desert sandstorm. Leavenworth left a lot of grit wherever he went, and not the kind of grit that gets you into a cowboy movie.

In his meaty hand, the color of sausage, he grasped a wad of papers, crinkled under his white-knuckled grip. As much as newspaper was in Curtis's blood, money was in Donald Leavenworth's. He was a bottom-line kind of man, intolerant of failure and unfortunately, ignorant of technology. Whatever he worked on, it was on printed paper. He still handwrote every letter or document. He didn't even have a computer in his office. His assistant had to manage all his e-mail.

So Curtis guessed that whatever was in his blood-boiling grip came from the Internet, which Mr. Leavenworth regarded as a personal enemy— as if the thing were alive, breathing and officing across the street.

"This is it, Macy. It's the end of the road for her. The end of the road."

Mr. Leavenworth's barrel chest heaved. His brow glistened in sweat. His eyes bulged just like his belly, contained by an overly taxed white shirt, filled to capacity with buttons threatening to pop and fly every direction across the room if he drew in a big breath. On anyone else, his ruddy, sweaty face would send alarm bells and calls to 911 for an impending heart attack. But this was Mr.

Leavenworth every day. His ghost-white hair was thinning by the hour. When he waddled briskly, which he always did, his hair stood straight up to reveal every liver spot on his scalp. He was a man who knew no other way except the way of the pressure cooker.

Curtis had always vowed to not die in his office like his grandfather, or lose his mind like his father. He loved the newspaper, but he had no ambitions to die for it. Not in its pathetic state, anyway. It had been another untimely passing that taught him life was too short to spend it working to death. Except now all he had was work. So the truth was, he spent most nights working late, trying to save a paper that wasn't his to save, from a world that devalued good reporting and instead thrived on the rumor mill that spread like wildfire in 140 characters or less.

He still did, and always would, value investigative reporting and the integrity of the long forgotten newspaper—what it could do to shape and mold a society that read it. That's what his father had taught him before he lost hope in his own mantra.

"Sir," Curtis began. His wife taught him to be diplomatic in an argument. That single talent had gotten him promoted three times at this paper alone. "Look, let's just--"

"You hired her. You get to fire her."

"Fire her?" Curtis leaned back into the back of his chair, hoping it would hold him steady. Mr. Leavenworth was a blowhard. He threatened a lot of things, but when he said *fired* that really was the end of the road. "Sir, Riley has a following. A good following."

Mr. Leavenworth was jabbing his finger toward the papers on the edge of Curtis's desk. "A following? Really? Take a look at *that*."

Curtis picked up the papers. "The blog," Curtis sighed.

"Is that what they're calling it these days? Because I'm calling it a knifing."

"Sir, you must understand. Anybody can start a blog. And blogs get lots of attention when they're controversial and mean-spirited."

"The problem, Macy, is that we're *not* getting lots of attention. They're turning on her."

Curtis quickly scanned the papers. He was familiar with this blog. It was an anonymous person ranting against all things romantic — all things Riley. Whoever this was ridiculed every one of Riley's columns. It oftentimes seemed personal. But Curtis gave no stock to someone who cowardly bashed another person's writings anonymously.

"Her latest article...*Life is Like the Movies*? Seriously? In today's cynical world, nobody believes that tripe." Mr. Leavenworth's index finger was pointed at nothing in particular. His other hand was balled up and punched into his hip. "We've got emails clogging the...the..." He looked to the ceiling for his answer.

"Mainframe."

"Yes. Mainframe. Complaining about it. We need a new column in there. Something fresh. Something that will sell me some newspapers!"

Curtis knew. They'd been steadily declining, while also losing every demographic under sixty. The Ask Riley column, though, had seemed to be the perfect solution. In a world obsessed with romance, she'd brought a fresh, vibrant and positive voice to the paper. And people seemed to love her. But Mr. Leavenworth was right. The world was increasingly becoming cynical. And its shallow take on commitment wasn't helping. Hardly anyone knew what commitment meant. What "for better or for worse" took. Truthfully, he didn't buy into Riley's take on romance, but he did what he had to do to sell papers.

With a careful hand, he adjusted Marie's picture he kept on his desk. She smiled back at him, frozen into a nice day at the beach. *Keep a cool head.* He came from a long line of men who had no history of restraint.

Curtis looked at Mr. Leavenworth. "Next week, I'm getting Riley on Caller Up."

"The national radio call-in show?" Though everything about him still bulged, he looked mildly impressed.

"That's the one. It's Valentine's Day week and she's the perfect guest. I'm certain this appearance will open up syndication opportunities." Curtis chose his words carefully, purposefully using syndication and opportunity in the same sentence.

Mr. Leavenworth's chest stopped heaving. Although the dullness in his eyes didn't leave, his features didn't look like they were melting off his face. On particularly stressful days, his mouth drooped nearly past his chin.

"You have 'til the end of next week to prove to me she's worth keeping." And then he was gone.

Curtis put his head in his hands. How could he fire Riley? It was like firing the sunshine and telling it you prefer the blue, ghostly, cold light of the moon.

"Mr. Macy…"

Curtis looked up as Miranda slipped into the office. She slid sideways through the door like it was a crack in the wall. Wherever she was, it seemed like she shouldn't be there. She whispered a lot, even about mundane things like the weather. She was a hard person to trust, Curtis found, because though he couldn't prove it, he always sensed there was an ulterior motive.

Curtis sat straight in his chair. "Miranda,

where is my storm water run-off article?" He put his hand on his desk phone. He always had to give Miranda some kind of prompt to indicate she shouldn't linger, because that's what she did, everywhere, was linger.

She tucked her long, straight, dark-as-a-cave hair behind her ears. She always wore bright lipstick, the kind of bright that causes spontaneous blinking. He never knew where to look when talking to her because she also had a habit of dressing in anything that plunged well below the neckline.

"It's coming," she said, lightly sitting on the arm of the chair that sat in front of his desk. "Listen, I was thinking. Give me a stab at a new--"

"Can it wait?" He kept his hand on the phone. "I've got something I need to take care of."

"It can wait," she said, her eyes narrow, "but by the sound of the conversation I heard while standing in the hallway waiting to talk to you, you don't have a lot of time to wait."

Curtis waved her off. "If you'll excuse me, I need to make a phone call."

As pulled together as Miranda usually was, when she didn't get her way, she skulked out of the room like a third grader, slumping in the exact way a woman wearing a plunging neckline shouldn't.

When she left, he flipped through his Rolodex and quickly dialed the number. As it rang, he stared at Marie and she stared back at him. He could do this for hours a day if he let himself.

"Caller Up, may I help you?"

"Yes, this is Curtis Macy from the *L.A. Tribune*. I need to speak with your station manager."

"Your business, sir?"

"I'm following up about booking the Ask Riley columnist for Valentine's Day."

"One moment."

Curtis let out a breath as she put him on hold. *Following up* was a bit of a stretch. He'd never made the first phone call. But his dad taught him that with some ingenuity, things could turn around pretty quickly. His dad frequently pulled deals together at the last minute, managing himself some memorable victories. But even at a young age, Curtis remembered it had also landed him in some dark corners. Emma Riley was about to find herself in a dark corner if he couldn't get her and her Ask Riley fame on this radio show. And quick.

Cheryl McKay (aka The Screenwriter)

Backstory Comparison (Sample H)
This scene comes from pg. 9-10 of the script and it's lifted from the second chapter of the novel. The reason we're showing you this in a chapter on backstory is the way Rene added lots of backstory to Curtis's character to introduce him. Coming from a long line of newspaper writers was not in the script, but it was a delightful addition to the novelized version of the story. The backstory about his wife is from the script and Rene preserved that by introducing it in slices, just like I did in the screenplay.

Even if I liked the backstory she added with Curtis's father and grandfather, I'm not sure where it would fit in the screenplay. If there were room for it, it would be much later in the script, perhaps in a scene between Curtis and Riley when she asks him questions about his past to get to know him better. But do I need it? Is it essential for telling the movie version of the story? Probably not.

As mentioned, one of my jobs as the screenwriter, when we are working on a novelization, is to help Rene not write herself into any corners early on in the project. I try to pay attention to any backstory she adds to make sure she's not putting anything in there that will cause unnecessary challenges for her later into the book. When we started on

Ask Riley, she initially wrote the same backstory for Curtis except it was this current paper his family worked for and not another. I knew for reasons deeper into the story that Curtis could not have worked at this location for more than three years. So we had to adjust that this wasn't the same newspaper the family started.

As a side note, did you notice Rene changed Mr. Quackenbush's name to Mr. Leavenworth? Rene felt that if the reader had to see that name over and over, it might read a bit cartoonish. In the movie, it probably wouldn't cause the viewer a second thought because it is just spoken a few times. But in book form, it'll be in there a few dozen times, so it was an artistic choice to change it.

Next, we'll look at a sample where a novel weaves in more backstory in the book opening than the screenplay does. The backstory added to the opening is revealed over time in the script, but in the novel slices of it come up front.

* * *

SAMPLE I

To follow are the opening two script pages from *Merry's Christmas: a love story* by Susan Rohrer: (Used by permission.)

EXT. TRAIN PLATFORM - CHICAGO - DAYBREAK

The EL rumbles by. CITY WORKERS wrap street lights with garland, heralding the Yuletide season.

MEREDITH "MERRY" HOPPER, late 20s, throws open the window of her underlying single apartment, her well-worn pajamas doing little to shield her from the winter blast. Merry calls over the train noise to her fastidious apartment super, MR. GRABINSKI, 60s, as he sweeps.

> MERRY
> Merry Christmas, Mr.
> Grabinski!

> GRABINSKI
> Merry, Schmerry. Barely
> picked up from Thanksgiving
> and already they got needles
> all over the walk.

Merry's eyes widen as she notices a TOW
TRUCK GUY hooking up an old rattle-trap red
Volkswagen Beetle at the curb.

> MERRY
> No! No, no, hey that's...
> Wait!

Merry ducks inside. Ragged curtains blow out
the abandoned open window. Grabinski grouses
after her.

> GRABINSKI
> The window! Merry! I'm not
> heating the whole free world!

INT. MERRY'S SINGLE APARTMENT - DAY

Merry dashes through her humble dwelling.
Makeshift Christmas decorations overflow an
old box on the table. Merry throws a coat on
and leaps over a CALICO CAT, RUDY.

> MERRY
> Wait, wait, wait... I'm
> coming!

EXT. LOW RENT APARTMENT BUILDING - DAY

Curbside, the tow truck guy secures Merry's
VW Beetle. Merry bursts out toward the
street.

                        MERRY
          Mister, please. I'm good for it!
          I get paid this afternoon.

                        TOW TRUCK GUY
          Then you can take it to
          the impound.

Merry chases the guy around his rig as he
boards it.

                        MERRY
          Come on, it's Christmas time.
          How am I supposed to get around?

                        TOW TRUCK GUY
          Sounds like the upside of
          living under a train.

                        MERRY
          Please. Okay, okay, just...
          Come on, look at me like a
          human being in genuine
          need and...don't do this.

                        TOW TRUCK GUY
          No, you look at me. I don't
          take the car, I don't get
          paid, then I got nothing to
          put under the tree for my kids
          this year.

                        MERRY
          But... Seriously? Kids, huh?
          Oh, just take it.

The guy pulls away, Merry's car bouncing
along behind him. Merry watches, defeated,
as her Bug disappears.

                    GRABINSKI
          Monday's the first. You got
          rent.

Merry pulls her coat closed and hurries back
inside.

                    MERRY
          I know, I know.

INT. MERRY'S SINGLE APARTMENT - DAY

Rudy (the cat) barely looks up as Merry
enters. She closes the door, choking back
tears.

                    * * *

To follow are the opening novel pages from *Merry's Christmas: a love story* by Susan Rohrer:

Perhaps it didn't make sense to throw open the window and let the scant heat of a drafty studio apartment escape into the brisk December air. But for Merry Hopper, responding to the fullness of her heart trumped what made sense to most other people on a regular basis.

No matter what anyone thought, said, or did, and most especially on this particular morning, everything in Merry sang out in celebration. This was the season — her season. She knew it, with a conviction as dependable as the elevated train rumbling by hourly, as certain as the rent she had no way to pay, and as insistent as the calico cat at her feet, meowing for breakfast.

"There they are, Rudy!" Merry scooped up the feline for a peek out the window. "Look. See? It's already starting."

Indeed, just across the street, city workers bustled about, fest ...ng the eaves of the train station with machine-wrought pine boughs and enormous extruded bows. Clearly, the decorations had weathered many a year, but the sight of their return was still a welcome reminder of the coming Yuletide season.

Even though Merry had been both born and abandoned on Christmas day almost twenty-nine years prior; even though she'd been bounced around the foster care system without ever having a family to call her own, Christmas was a time when Merry liked to think that all the world was celebrating her birthday, too. Jubilantly, she threw open the sash.

"Merry Christmas, Mr. Grabinski!" Merry called out, the winter blast whipping through her well-worn pajamas.

Fastidious to a fault, the apartment super barely looked up at her. "Merry Schmerry." He continued to sweep balsam and pine bits into compulsive little piles on the walk. "I'm barely picked up from Thanksgiving and already they got needles all over creation."

Suddenly, Merry's eyes widened incredulously. It couldn't be happening, but it was. Just beyond Mr. Grabinski, a stocky, middle-aged man leaned over the business end of a tow truck. He was well into hooking up a faded red Volkswagen Beetle.

To call the vintage Bug red was, at most, a generous way of acknowledging what the color once was, long before the oxidation and saltings of too many Chicago winters had had their way with the paint. Still, it was Merry's — almost paid for with her meager base as a waitress. It would be all hers in just a couple of months, if holiday tipping measured up to her hopes.

"No! No, no, hey that's... Wait!" Merry ducked inside, disappearing from the window. Tattered curtains billowed out of the abandoned portal.

"The window, Merry! I'm not heating the whole free world!"

Hearing him, Merry circled back to close the window, and then dashed through her humble dwelling. She scrambled to throw on a coat that had seen far too many seasons, knocking an overflowing box of decorations onto the floor in the process.

"Wait, wait, wait... I'm coming!" Merry shouted, as she leapt over her calico cat, Rudy, and ran out of her apartment door, down the stairs, and out the front door.

At curbside, the tow truck guy continued to secure Merry's Beetle to his rig, undeterred by her protests. He hoisted the front end so the wheels left the ground.

Merry skidded to a stop. "Mister, please, I'm good for it. I get paid this afternoon."

"Then you can take it to the impound." He pulled up the waistband of his sagging pants.

"Come on, it's Christmas time. How am I supposed to get around?"

The expression on his face told Merry that this guy had heard it all. What was worse, he refused to look at her. "Sounds like the upside of living under a train." In a snap, he had locked off the car.

Merry was well accustomed to dealing with grouchy men. She had a way of breaking through the even gruffest of hearts to the soft, gooey center underneath. "Please." Merry paused. "Okay, okay, just... Come on, look at me like a human being in completely genuine need and don't do this."

Finally, he turned to her. For a moment, it seemed he might relent. "No, you look at me." He pointed greasy fingers toward himself. "I don't take the Bug, I don't get paid, then I got nothin' at all to put under the tree for my kids this year."

Merry stopped in her tracks. She had a soft spot for kids, especially kids who had to do without, the way she'd had to do for so many years. "But..." Merry continued, her conviction to fight for herself waning as the man headed toward the cab of his truck. She followed him as he plopped into the driver's seat and stuck his keys in the ignition. "Seriously? Kids, huh?"

"Five."

Suddenly, everything in Merry flip-flopped. She did look at the tow truck guy. She looked at him hard. He didn't seem nearly as heartless as he had at first. He wasn't her enemy. He was just a dad, working a thankless job in a tough economy to put food on the table for his family.

"Just take it." Merry heaved a sigh.

And take Merry's car, he did. Without another word, he started the truck and puttered away with Merry's not-so-very-red Beetle bouncing along in tow behind him.

Merry's face fell as the only thing of value she almost owned disappeared into the distance. It was like losing a friend of sorts, and she promised herself that somehow she'd get it back.

Merry turned. Despite the cold, heat flashed to her cheeks. Mr. Grabinski had observed the entire incident. He narrowed his gaze at her. "Monday's the first. You got rent."

She drew her coat close. "I know, I know."

Merry scurried back to her apartment and closed the door, choking back tears. Her cat, Rudy, studied her. He was that special kind of animal that seemed to understand when her life got to be overwhelming.

* * *

Cheryl McKay (aka The Screenwriter)

Backstory Comparison (Sample I)

Susan Rohrer's novelization of her screenplay, *Merry's Christmas*, illustrates how revealing backstory within the action of a scene can help you get to know a character better in a novel than in the script. There is more revealed about Merry in the opening of this novel than the script, even though both are by the same writer. You learn the same information in the screenplay, too, but some of that is layered throughout future scenes.

Here are some examples of what we learn in the novel opening that we do not learn yet in the script: Merry was a Christmas baby, she was abandoned, and Christmas is her favorite time of year. We also learn she is used to dealing with grouchy men.

We get to spend more time with her response to the tow truck driver having kids. You immediately like her because she puts the needs of these kids she doesn't know above herself. There is a hint of this in the script through Merry's reaction to his mention of the kids: "Just take it." It's revealed in the subtext of that dialogue. The novel version is more direct. It also gives us a peek into how she felt as a child, identifying with these kids who are in danger of having nothing.

The dialogue and structure of the novelization are mostly the same as the script, but the character-revealing backstory is what makes the scene play differently in novel form. The author has effectively used backstory to give us a peek into this character and helped us get to know Merry quicker.

Backstory Exercise

Take the following script pages from one of Cheryl's scripts, *According to Plan*, and highlight all the lines where you see backstory revealed in the script about AJ's character. Then we will give you a novelization exercise with the scene:

EXT. WELLINGTON HOME — DAY

Flowers bloom around an opulent home. The
yard's grass as vibrant as green can get, as
only Southern California can sport this time
of year. A Happy New Year flag flaps in the
wind by the front door.

Dandelions are clutched by a small hand,
some yellow, some white, ready for the
breath of a child to send their feather-like
seeds into the wind.

An adorable, energetic ball of feist, 6-year
old, MCKINLEY WELLINGTON, blows on one,
smiling as its seeds float around. She tilts
her face toward the sun, basking in its
glow.

She wears a white princess dress, which
curiously looks like a mini wedding gown.
She holds the rest of her dandelions in
front of her like they are a bridal bouquet
and walks across the grass, barefoot, as
though she is a bride.

                    MCKINLEY
                  (sing songy)
          Dah, dum, dum, dum. Dah,
          dum--

                    AJ
          McKinley!

The girl looks toward the source
interrupting her playtime:

The best-aunt-in-the-world-ever, according
to this child, stands at the top of the
steps to the front door. She's ALIYA JOY
MALONE, 28, affectionately known as AJ.

AJ is good-hearted, adorably clumsy at times, an encourager by nature, pretty much afraid of everything, and on the north side of the A.D.D. charts.

> AJ
> What is Princess McKinley
> doing outside of her castle?
> I thought we were going to
> build you a tower.

McKinley glides in wedding march fashion toward AJ.

> MCKINLEY
> Mommy always says I should
> practice to be good at
> something.

> AJ
> And what skill are we
> perfecting?

> MCKINLEY
> The march. For your
> wedding. Auntie AJ, I have
> to be completely prepared.

> AJ
> That would come in oh, so
> handy, if I were, you know,
> getting married.

> MCKINLEY
> You are. Maybe not today.
> But you are.

> AJ
> Oh, honey. I haven't been on
> a date since eleventh grade, so
> I wouldn't save a block on
> your calendar anytime soon.

McKinley arrives at AJ's feet, uses her
index finger in that "come here" motion to
prompt AJ to bend down to her level. They
stare each other down, eye-to-eye. McKinley
takes her aunt's face in her hands:

>   MCKINLEY
>   You will. And when you do,
>   I am wearing this, my
>   princess costume, as your
>   dandelion girl.

>   AJ
>   McKinley, you might grow out
>   of that by the time you play
>   flower girl for me.

McKinley harrumphs, her face pouty.

>   AJ (CONT'D)
>   You may even get married
>   before I do.

>   MCKINLEY
>   Oh, poopie feathers. Have a
>   little faith.

>   AJ
>   Faith has nothing to do with
>   it, kiddo. You know you're
>   carrying weeds?

>   MCKINLEY
>   Dandelions. They're my favorite.

>   AJ
>   Doesn't cancel the weed
>   factor. No bride picks weeds
>   for her wedding. I'm surprised
>   you could even find a batch in
>   my sister's yard.

                    MCKINLEY
                   (whispers)
      I stole them from the neighbor's.

                      AJ
              (copies her whisper)
      They pay people to take those away.

                    MCKINLEY
      Then you won't have to arrest me.

                      AJ
      I'm not a cop yet. But I'll
      send grandpa over with his
      cuffs. Now, go in before your
      mother accuses me of letting
      you play in the dirt in that
      dress.

McKinley tosses what's left of her flowers
in the yard, hikes up her dress and heads up
the stairs toward the front door.

                    MCKINLEY
      Yeah, yeah. But I have a plan.
      I am finding you a Valentine.
      It's my New Year's resolution.

                      AJ
      How about you find me a job
      first? Full salary? Pension
      plan? Paid time off for
      good behavior?

                    MCKINLEY
      I don't need to. Because this
      time, Auntie AJ, you are going
      to pass your shooting test.

                      AJ
      You taking over your momma's
      job as my life coach?

```
The child smiles, obviously believes in AJ
to the max.

                    MCKINLEY
          Remember.  Just picture your
          success first, and you'll be
          fine.

AJ is not so sure. As she watches her niece
go inside, apprehension grows on her face.
```

                              * * *

Check your backstory list for AJ against mine. You may have highlighted a few additional things, but here are some essential elements that should definitely be highlighted:

1. AJ hasn't had a date since eleventh grade.
2. AJ is not about to get married and doesn't have a lot of faith that the single season of her life will end anytime soon.
3. AJ wants to be a cop but isn't yet. She has a test coming up to try to become one. The word "this time" by McKinley implies backstory that she has tried to pass before but didn't prevail.
4. Her father is a cop.
5. She's unemployed and needs a job.
6. Her sister acts as her life coach and appears to live a much more successful life.

For the assignment, use AJ's POV to write your version of a novel opening. Notice this means the opening—where it seems the child is alone—will need AJ added to the scene, perhaps observing McKinley, if you want to include those details. While in a movie version, AJ won't be in the scene until halfway down the page, that won't work in the novel.

Take your favorite piece (or pieces) of backstory that are in the scene and inflate them. Pick your favorite angle, and tell us more details about her history. Don't tell us all the details about her backstory. Whatever else is hinted at in dialogue could come out later in the story.

Here are some approaches you could take: What was that last date like in eleventh grade? What was so disastrous that she hasn't been on one since? What was it like the last time she tried to pass the test to get into the police academy? What was her last life coaching session like with her sister, given the current state of her life not going so well? Those are just a few examples of the types of areas you could expand. There are many to choose from. You could choose one for this opening, and save other elaborations for later into the story.

You could do this exercise more than once and choose to focus on different parts of her history for different versions. See which one you like best. Which one makes you care most about AJ as a character and draws you in the fastest? Naturally, you don't want to unload all the backstory at once. It should be unpeeled over time, just like it would be if you went to see the movie. You can keep some of those hints in the dialogue, but choose to explore through AJ's thoughts one or two significant aspects.

And here's another challenge: How would your backstory introduction of AJ change if you knew her last date in eleventh grade was with her brother-in-law, McKinley's father? Yes, the one her sister married after he dumped AJ for her sister, Natalia. Would you reveal that here or wait until later into the story? Would you hint at it here?

The creative choices of writers are limitless. It's a matter of choosing what you feel is best.

Next up, we will talk about characters.

Chapter Eight

CHARACTERS

Rene Gutteridge (aka The Novelist)

Questions to Ask about Characters
If the screenwriter has done her job, the characters are already established. Now, there can be some need for adjustments here and there. But overall, having the characters already established has been one way I have been able to lean on the screenwriter's prior work. Establishment of characters, along with structure and plot discussed earlier, are two of the biggest areas that make writing a novelization easier than creating a new novel from scratch.

To follow are the types of questions a novelist can ask when figuring out the landscape of the characters to adapt from script to book:

1. **Do I need to cut characters?** Typically, I do not need to cut characters. In fact, a novel adapted for screen is more likely to lose characters. Characters don't cost a novelist anything. The only reason to not include a script character is if that character is a part of a storyline you don't plan to include in the novel.

2. **Do I need to combine characters?** Again, this would be rare. There's a lot more room in novels for characters than in scripts, but there

are always exceptions to the rule.

3. **Do I need to add characters?** This is a more common experience, especially if you need someone for your POV character to talk to. It's also common if you're creating backstory that is not in the script. Then you will have to add characters here and there.

4. **Do I need to make a character's role bigger or smaller than it is in the script?** In a novelization, you're almost always making roles bigger because you're expanding the storyline.

5. **Do I need to change any of the characterizations, personalities, or motives established by the screenwriter?** This will be at your discretion, and it will depend on how you tell the story. A lot of change stems from the POV character choices. An example: when I wrote *Heart of the Country*, I was in the POV of a character that in the script would've been considered a secondary character. Because she had a bigger role in the book, I had to give her more established motivations and even put her in a scene that she wasn't originally a part of in the script.

There are also questions a novelist should ask the screenwriter before starting a project that may make the job easier:

1. **What backstory did you have in mind when you wrote your lead characters?**

2. **Is there something in the subtext you want to make sure I understand?**

3. Do any of the side characters have any significant backstories?

4. Do you have a sequel or prequel already planned that may affect how I write a particular character's story or backstory?

5. What actor or actress did you picture in the main roles?   (If the movie is already in production, make sure you find out who is cast.)

Let me share one example where I expanded a character. Early on when I read the script for *Heart of the Country*, I grew attached to the character of the mom. Although she is mostly just referred to in the script, I decided to expand her character in the book because I felt her storyline caused the crisis of an entire family. It was a great way to add additional words and scenes for the book, *and* give the reader a wider glimpse into the story. So much has to be cut in a film, but in novels, as we've said, we have the luxury of more room. But the great thing about this choice was that it always brought the story back to its central points and central characters. So it didn't take away from the initial story. Rather, it added to it while keeping it on point.

* * *

Cheryl McKay (aka The Screenwriter)

Characters from Script to Book
There will be characters who will end up with histories the screenwriter never considered. And that's okay! It's one of the fun parts of being the screenwriter, watching your characters come to life in new ways. As screenwriters, we usually don't need to write long, historical biographies on each of our characters before we start writing our scripts. But if you did write any biographies or character traits lists

or backstories that aren't explicit in the script, you are welcome to provide that information to your novelist. It could serve as a great jumping off point for her so she knows what you had in mind.

A novelist may want to draw from the character's backstory to create a character that isn't in the script. For example, when penning the script for *Never the Bride*, I wrote that Jessie had a history of having an imaginary friend when she was nine years old. We find out in conversations there was a psychiatrist, Dr. Montrose, who counseled this "friend" out of her. I did not have this doctor in the present-day story, just the past. Rene decided to add him to the present and have Jessie go talk to him about her current "potentially imaginary friend" named God. We ended up with a great chapter that deepened Jessie's character, as she had to face this doctor's difficult questions about God and faith. Would God show up and offer to write a girl's love story, like Jessie had posed? I loved the chapter Rene wrote so much, I wrote a three-paged scene and put it in the script. This was our biggest change from novel back to script. It's a great example of when Rene wasn't veering off in her own direction, coming up with something that had nothing to do with the original story. Yet it was still fresh and a wonderful change. She put a character from the lead character's history into the present, and it worked brilliantly.

Next, let's look at a sample from *Greetings from the Flipside*. We will include a short opening scene from the script that was later worked into a new sequence in the novel that did not come from the screenplay.

* * *

SAMPLE J

INT. FIRST GRADE CLASS - DAY (TWENTY-FIVE YEARS AGO)

SIX-YEAR-OLDS finger paint. Most of them CHATTER LOUDLY with each other. A GIRL IN PIGTAILS concentrates on her painting, a different color on each finger.

HER PAINTING shows a clear picture of a mother, father and child. For a six-year old, she paints well.

An AWKWARD BOY in Coke-bottle glasses slides up to her desk, his newly painted project done. With a beaming smile, he hands her the paper: it's folded in half like a handmade card.

He giggles and ducks away, embarrassed. A TEACHER watches him with a smile of her own. This is too cute.

The Girl in Pigtails looks over the card, leaving her paint-covered fingerprints on it.

The front has two stick-figures holding hands: one girl, one boy. She flips it open: Inside it says "DO YOU LIKE ME? CHECK IN THE BOX: YES, NO, MAYBE SO."

                                    SMASH CUT TO:

The card slapped onto the little boy's desk.

                    GIRL IN PIGTAILS
              Okay, so, this is cliché.
              It needs more than stick
              thingys.
                        (MORE)

```
            GIRL IN PIGTAILS (CONT'D)
      They have zero personality,
      expression. And inside,
      you're asking me to make
      a choice but you don't
      say what you think. We
      need a rewrite.
```

The expert card writer stalks off with her head held high.

The Teacher gives the Awkward Boy a sympathetic smile. It looks like he might cry. But then, a crooked smile grows.

The spunky girl's eyes focus on her drawing.

* * *

To follow is the corresponding novel sequence from Chapter Two of *Greetings from the Flipside*:

Jake tried not to seem too obvious as he watched Mrs. Dungard's expression. He lifted the bouquet from below the counter, handing it over like it was a newborn baby. But it was the expressions that always made his day. Mrs. Dungard's whole face opened in delight, her eyes shining with pure joy as she grappled for words.

"Oh, Jake! You've outdone yourself this time!" Her fingers delicately stroked the petals of the Egyptian lotus, which he'd encircled with some baby's breath.

"It's called the Sacred Lily of the Nile," Jake said. "They were grown along the Nile thousands of years ago and the Egyptians ate their roots, which were edible."

"The color is astounding. And I love how it's all wrapped in lilies! Susan will love these! Did I tell you it's her birthday?"

"You did." Jake smiled. "And I also remembered, from last year, that hot pink is her favorite color."

Mrs. Dungard's eyes shone with tears. She patted Jake on the hand. "You don't know how much this means to me."

He did know. He always knew that a simple bouquet of flowers could reset a fractured relationship, bring hope to something hopeless, say a thousand things without whispering a word.

"How is Susan doing?"

"She's holding her own. But the chemo is taking its toll." Jake went around the counter to the small rack of handmade cards he kept in the shop, usually only ten or fifteen at a time. He pulled the one showcasing summer, a field of yellow flowers in the distance that perfectly matched the setting sun. He'd written the poem inside himself.

"Take this and give it to her too."

"Thank you, Jake. Your cards are so beautiful." She cradled the bouquet. "Thank you so much for this too. It's just breathtaking."

"You're welcome."

Mrs. Dungard left and Jake closed the shop for the evening. He liked this time of day, when the sun was settling to bed and the shop was quiet.

He closed the register and found Mindy, his assistant, in the back.

"Hey Mindy, you can go on home."

"But we've still got a lot to do for the wedding this weekend," she said as she measured some ribbon.

"I'll finish it up."

"You're sure?"

"Definitely. Go home and see that baby girl of yours." He grinned extra wide to let her know it was okay. Mindy tended to feel guilty about doing things for herself.

She grabbed her bag. "I'm nervous about this one. The mother is kind of . . . strange, I guess you could say. She's the same lady that has us send that Columbine flower to the nursing home every day, right?"

It was true. She wanted it every day. And when their driver was sick, he took the flower himself.

"Yes."

"She was having a hard time articulating what her daughter wanted, or I was having a hard time understanding. Either way . . . I'm nervous."

"No worries. I already have an idea what to do."

Relief flooded Mindy's features. "You rock, Jake. Seriously. You never fail. Why was I worried?"

"See you tomorrow."

Alone in the back room he sat on his favorite old stool, the one his father had carved for him when he was ten years old, and began his final sketch of the bouquet. She wasn't frilly. Or girly. But she was feminine and pretty. Tough but vulnerable. At least, that's how he remembered her.

A lot of his youthful memories had faded, but he would never in his life forget the day he gave Hope Landon a card in the first grade. It was Mrs. Mosley's class.

It had taken every nerve he had to do it. The night before, with a flashlight under his covers, he wrote the card, practicing good penmanship and making sure he spelled the important words correctly. The next day in class he'd managed to add some crayon to it, for a final touch. Then he stuffed it down his pants to hide it from Mrs. Mosley — in hindsight, possibly a mistake.

Then it was time. Art class. They were painting spring cards. He was watching her from across the room as she fervently worked, as if the whole world depended on the card she was creating. Her passion — and her dimples — fascinated him.

He finished his spring card in five minutes, which he intended for his mother, and started painting the easel itself. If caught, no recess for him.

Admittedly, he was just delaying because he was nervous. This was the first girl that hadn't grossed him out.

He was a scrawny thing with big magnifier glasses and wispy hair that even back then seemed too old for him. High-priced hair gel couldn't hide the fact that even at seven his hair was receding like the tide on the shoreline.

He watched her and then, she stopped painting. Her hand rested on her knee, the paintbrush poking out between two fingers. She slumped a little, observing whatever it was she was painting. In one spectacular moment, he'd found a burst of confidence. He stood and walked to her with a strut he'd only seen on TV, his shoulders back, his chin tipped upward enough to make him at least an inch taller, he estimated.

Then came the sudden realization, only four feet away from her, that he'd forgotten to take the card out of his pants. He had to think fast. And he did. Halfway through his stride, he turned, pulled it out, kept walking.

Very smooth.

But with each step closer, his confidence faded. By the time he got to her, he was shaking. But she didn't notice. She didn't even look at him. He cleared his throat. Nothing.

There he stood. It was a very Charlie Brown moment.

So he dropped the card in her lap and ran off.

To his surprise, forty minutes later during free time in their class, she stood by his desk. "I appreciate the thought," she said, towering over him. "But this is cliché." He didn't know what that word meant. She slapped the card down on his desk and opened it up. "See here? *Do you like me? Yes, no, maybe so.* The rhyming is good, but I think you can do better. Something funny, like 'Do you like me? I also come in chocolate and strawberry.' Girls like boys who are funny. Also, you're not telling me how you *feel* about me." She grabbed his pencil and pointed to the front of the card. "And stick figures? At least give them expression. Personality. Enthusiasm. It's got to catch my eye."

And that was the end of it. She walked off and never checked a box.

But she never stopped being his Lucy, either. By the time they got to their senior year of high school, he was pretty sure she didn't even recognize him anymore.

And now, he was arranging flowers for her wedding. Bittersweet, to say the least. She probably didn't even know it was him. Her mother was the one who came in and made all the arrangements.

No matter. His life was not one he wanted to share anymore. But he was going to give her the most beautiful bouquet he'd ever designed. She deserved that. His whole young life, she stood out as the girl who deserved better than what she had.

His pencil flowed over the paper. Two hours later, he was still working.

Cheryl McKay (aka The Screenwriter)

Character Comparison (Sample J)
Mrs. Dungard and Mindy are new characters, exclusive to the book only. In my script, I established that Jake was doing the flowers for Hope's wedding and that they had a history together, where she didn't like his card and rewrote

it. I didn't need the scene at the flower shop.

By showing the flower shop, Rene needed to create a couple of characters: the customer and then Mindy, who recurs throughout the novel and is a lovely addition to the story. Rene was careful to make sure Mindy wasn't like any of the characters I had created, in personality, so she added to the story as a whole. Rene worked in my flashback scene to establish Hope and Jake's backstory. However, notice this is not the opening of the book like it is for the screenplay. Rene still used it, but put it in a scene that didn't exist in the screenplay.

Character Exercise
For screenwriters, make a list of your most important characters. Write up biographies on your characters from traits, to backstory, to personality quirks. This is a tool you can give a novelist to adapt your script.

For novelists, if you are novelizing a script, write up a list of questions you want to ask the screenwriter about their main characters, their personalities and motivations.

If you aren't presently working on a particular project, reread the scene from *According to Plan* in the prior chapter on backstory. Write up a character biography for AJ's character based on the information you gleaned from the slices revealed about her personality and backstory. Try to come up with some interesting details about her past and how that affects who she is today.

Next we will look at the translation of script dialogue and character voices into novel form.

Chapter Nine
DIALOGUE & VOICES

Cheryl McKay (aka The Screenwriter)

Voices of the Characters

When a novelist adapts a script into a novel, one area they should be able to lean on the screenwriter for is in the establishment of character voices. Hopefully, that screenwriter has done her job in coming up with a different voice for each character. Because the voices of certain characters will bleed through to the narrative (for those who get to be point of view characters), the novelist can use the voice established in the script. They can inspire the way the novelist writes the interior monologue. If a character is snarky in her dialogue, she should retain this snarky humor in the interior monologue, perhaps even more so. This is a creative decision the novelist can come to when establishing the storyteller(s) point(s) of view.

When choosing various point of view characters, each chapter will have a different tone and feel because of that character's voice, both how he sounds in his mind as well as the voice that is established in dialogue.

Dialogue of the Characters

When adapting scripts, novelists will also face decisions about what dialogue works and what needs to change. This is especially true when needing to combine scenes or rearrange the order or structure of scenes. They should also feel free to let their inspiration guide them if something sounds better rewritten, expanded, shortened, etc. They also may need to add dialogue to one scene if another scene was cut. For example, if a script scene has to be cut because there is no point of view character in it, that same information needs to come out in a different way in a different scene. So dialogue from various scenes can merge into one.

One fun area for a novelist in an adaptation is the play between text and subtext. Screenwriters hope their subtext comes through in the actors' performances and how directors interpret lines. Yet a novelist can tell you the subtext, often humorously, in how the words spoken to another character are opposite of what the character is thinking privately.

* * *

Rene Gutteridge (aka The Novelist)

How Novelists use Script Dialogue
Dialogue is one of the easiest parts of the novelization, mostly because dialogue is the screenwriter's main tool in the craft. Screenwriters are typically (or at least should be) masters of dialogue. Their dialogue has to serve multiple purposes and must say and do everything they need it to. A novelist has the luxury of helping the reader along by adding interior monologue, description, hand and body gestures and more. The screenwriter must form dialogue that speaks for itself.

So, rarely do I change the dialogue from script to novel. Mostly I use it as a jumping-off point. Because scenes move faster and are shorter in film, I take the script's dialogue and expand on it. Sometimes I'll add to the front, if I feel the passage needs more establishment, and I almost always add onto the back, to close out the scene. If I need a scene to be bigger for me, I might even add dialogue to the middle. But of all the adaptation challenges in novelizations, dialogue is the least challenging. For me, it's the place where I get to play the most. I take the screenwriter's stretch of dialogue and add action, interior monologue, description, and more. I always think of it as a sandbox where I get to dig for little treasures. It is where I get to hear the character speak and learn his or her voice.

As Cheryl mentioned, I like to play a lot with contradictions in dialogue and interior monologue. It's fun when a character speaks one thing, but the reader (through interior monologue) knows the character is feeling or thinking something different. What a task that is for an actor, to convey contradiction between the inner and outer man! Luckily, novelists have a whole toolbox from which to accomplish this.

Because novelists have the luxury of time that screenwriters don't, dialogue can be a great way to add to the story. The challenge is to mimic the original voice of each character, the voice the screenwriter created. If she created a shy and timid character, who is utterly afraid to speak in front of a crowd of more than two, not only does your additional dialogue need to match that, but your interior monologue should as well.

Because a screenplay is, in essence, a blueprint for a movie, the novelist must also create the world that exists around the dialogue. She needs to fill in the empty spaces that would ordinarily be filled by the director, the props, the setting, etc. It is how we weave dialogue into the novel that sets it apart from the screenplay.

So, my advice for dialogue is to have a lot of fun playing with the device that makes screenwriters shine.

In the following sample, Cheryl will walk you through a script-to-novel example of how dialogue and voices were adapted from *Greetings from the Flipside*.

* * *

SAMPLE K

To follow is from the *Greetings from the Flipside* script:

EXT. CICI'S HOME — NIGHT

Hope carries her wedding dress, wrapped in plastic, up to the front of a tiny, quaint house. She lives with Mom.

INT. CICI'S HOME - LIVING AREA - NIGHT

This place hasn't been redecorated since the seventies. Paisley print couch cover, shag carpet. Lots of rusts, yellows, and lime greens. CICI, 60s, Hope's kooky mother, sits at the table putting together silk flower arrangements. The ribbons don't match.

                    CICI
          Hello, dear dear. When I make
          the pigs in a blanket, do you
          want Swiss or provolone?
          I'm thinking cheddar.

                    HOPE
          Please tell me you finally
          got the travel documents from
          whatever this surprise
          honeymoon is.

Cici leaps up, grabs an envelope from a travel agency.

                    CICI
          They came today.

Hope takes the envelope.

                    HOPE
          Finally. So, are we going
          somewhere tropical?

Cici smiles in anticipation as Hope pulls out the contents. Two plane tickets to IDAHO and a B&B flier.

                    HOPE (CONT'D)
          Idaho? We're spending our
          honeymoon in potato country.

                    CICI
          That B&B harvests their own
          potatoes.

                    HOPE
          Great. Is this refundable?

                    CICI
          Nope. But it's paid in full!

Cici runs her hand down the side of Hope's
head.

                    CICI (CONT'D)
          You're going to look so
          pretty in that veil. If your
          father shows up, how 'bout
          we both take an arm?

                    HOPE
          Okay, Mom.

Cici grabs Hope's hands, pulls her
involuntarily into a prayer. Cici has what
is best described as the spontaneous prayer
version of Tourette's. Plus, she's loud.

                    CICI
          Lord, please hear this, our
          prayer. Bring Hope's daddy back
          in time for her vows. Thank you
          in advance, one thousand times two.

Hope heads into the connected kitchen.

                    CICI (CONT'D)
          And please convince Hope and
          Sam they don't need to move away.

Hope reemerges with a blue freezer pop.

                    HOPE
          Good night, Mom. Love you.

Hope swings out of the room.

INT. HOPE'S BEDROOM - NIGHT

On her twin bed, with her cell phone to her
ear, Hope listens to the last of her
fiancé's voice greeting as she curls the
corner of a PHOTO OF HER FATHER smiling, by
himself.

                    SAM (O.S.)
          So, I'm probably off playing
          some awesome gig right now. But
          if you're important, maybe I'll
          ring you.

There's a GUITAR RIFF before the standard
BEEP. Hope looks at her engagement ring as
she leaves her message.

                    HOPE
          Hi, Sam. It's me. I love you and
          can't wait to walk down that aisle.
           (realizing her sappiness)
          ...and not live in Poughkeepsie
          anymore with shag carpeting.
          Lime green walls. You know what?
          Just delete this message.

She disconnects the call, sits a quiet
moment on her bed.

                    HOPE (CONT'D)
          Me. I'm getting married.

She SQUEALS happily then accidentally slips
off the bed.

To follow are sample pages from *Greetings from the Flipside: a novel*:

Hope found her mother at the kitchen table, still surrounded by mustard yellow chairs that came in and out of style all in the same year: 1975. Her mother was dumping a sack of fake flowers and mismatched ribbon out onto the table. Hope sat down with the kind of caution that is normally reserved for people in dangerous occupations like alligator wrestling or rattlesnake wrangling or customer service.

"Look what I bought! It was all on sale. Clearanced at ninety percent off! I figured we could use it somehow at the wedding. We must have some decor at your wedding."

At the word *decor*, Hope's attention drifted to the rust-colored walls of the kitchen. It was still unclear in what year the color had been popular. In the living room, the paisley print couch sat atop a green shag carpet. On the end tables were two lamps she swore came straight from the set of *The Brady Bunch*.

Her mom hadn't updated anything since 1979, including herself. Everything about her— from her frizzy, unkempt hair to her polyester floral skirt— seemed a bit faded, like an old photo. Hope watched as her mom continued to rummage through her craft store goodies. As she often did, she imagined they were having a normal conversation, a conversation any mother and daughter might have before a wedding. She'd done this since she was little, sit close to her mother and pretend they were conversing about school or boys or an upcoming dance. That made her feel better. That . . .

And Popsicles.

"When I make the pigs in a blanket, do you

want Swiss or provolone? I'm thinking cheddar."

"Cheddar is fine." It was the pigs in a blanket that worried her. She'd agreed to let her mother cater only because there were no other options. They couldn't afford to have it professionally done, and their circle of friends was only about an inch across, thanks to her mother's unusual outlook on life.

On the brighter side, her mother had agreed they could pay a florist to do her bouquet and a few other arrangements. She was looking forward to seeing what he was planning. Rumor was that he always sketched out his bouquets before designing them, to get the client approval. It made her feel like she was from Spakenkill.

"So provolone?" her mother asked.

With her mother catering, she feared her wedding might look more like a backyard barbecue, complete with American flags and sparklers if she happened to find them in a discount bin somewhere.

Her mother chattered on about the pigs in a blanket, and Hope grabbed one of the ribbons, running it through her fingers. So much rode on her mother and Hope knew all too well that things dependent upon her mom were in a world of trouble. Hope bit her lip, desperately wanting to ask the same question she'd asked for four weeks now. But why would she assume the answer would be different this time?

Except Hope always seemed to live up to her name.

"Mom, did the travel documents come yet?" She held her breath.

Her mother blinked, as if trying to remember what a travel document was.

"For whatever this surprise honeymoon is that you've been talking about." Well, Mom mentioned it only once, but that was enough to get Hope's hope up.

"Documents! Yes!" Her mother jumped from the chair and hurried to the kitchen. "Came today!" She returned, clutching an envelope close to her heart, gazing at Hope with her head tilted to the side. She said nothing, just stared at Hope like she was a famous monument.

A tinge of excitement rose up in Hope and she couldn't help it: a grin hit her face like it was catapulted there. "So . . . are we going somewhere tropical?"

Her mother smiled and handed her the envelope.

Hope ripped it open, snatching up the folded contents. Tickets! Actual airline tickets! She turned them over to try to find the destination. A thrill rushed through her as she read the destination.

Then read it again.

Hope slowly lowered the tickets, placing them on the table.

Idaho.

The state.

The place nobody would go to for an exotic honeymoon. Her grin was still slapped onto her expression, but it began to quiver. She was about to burst into tears, but she had to hold it in. Crying extracted the strangest of all her mother's behaviors.

"It's a bed and breakfast!" her mother stated, her enthusiastic expression equivalent to Oprah's when she gives away new cars. "That B and B harvests *their own potatoes!*"

"We're spending our honeymoon in potato country."

"I know how much you love your mashed potatoes."

"Is this refundable?"

"Nope! Paid in full, my dear!" She smiled, missing the grave disappointment sinking into Hope's expression. Her mother started messing with the ribbon again.

What was there to say? She couldn't be ungrateful. She was certain her mother saved for months for this. A sharp pain cramped her stomach. Her mother reached across the table, patted her hand, grinned widely enough for the two of them.

"By the way, if your daddy shows up at the wedding, how about we both take an arm?"

No. Not now. Not talk about Daddy. "Sure, Mom."

Then the dim mood of the room was undone by what could only be described as the spontaneous prayer version of Tourette's syndrome. "Lord! Please hear this our prayer!" Her mother shouted, like there was some racket she needed to be heard over. She waved one hand in the air. "Bring Hope's daddy back in time for her vows!"

Her mother's eyes were squeezed shut so Hope rose, went to the freezer, and grabbed a blue Popsicle. She'd gone through ten or twelve Popsicles a day when her dad left. Now she only needed them every once in a while . . . like now. They had a calming effect, maybe because they temporarily froze her brain.

"Bring her daddy home, dear Lord!"

Hope returned to the table, sat down, sucked on her Popsicle.

"And please, please, please Lord, convince Hope and Sam they don't need to move away."

Hope's heart sank. Her mother was having a hard time with it, and it kind of broke her heart. But she needed to leave. She had to.

"It's going to be okay, Mom," Hope said, patting her on the hand. "I'm tired. I'm going to go to bed. Goodnight. I love you."

In her bedroom, against her will, she picked up the picture of her dad, the one where he grinned like he could see their whole future together and it was magnificent. It was winter, they were bundled tightly together, he had a thick mustache that was popular in the late seventies. Sideburns too. She always wondered what he'd look like in the current time, whether he'd have that mustache or not.

"I'm not going to get any silly ideas about you coming to the wedding," she said to the photograph. "There's a new man in my life now. He is my family. He is the one that will be there tomorrow. Not you." She tossed the frame aside and grabbed her cell phone, speed-dialing the man who would take her away from this place, forever.

His voice mail picked up. "Hey, it's Sam. I'm probably off playing some outrageously sick gig right now. But if you're important, maybe I'll ring you." A guitar vamp roared through the phone, followed by a delicate beep.

"Hey, it's me. I love you and can't wait to walk down the aisle. I can't wait to hear the song you're writing for me. I can't wait" — she glanced at the picture of her dad on the bedspread, still grinning — "to not live in Poughkeepsie anymore . . ." She was talking as if the voice mail might converse back. "You know what, I'm just rambling now. I've got lots to do, so I'll catch ya on the flipside."

Outside her room, her mother sang some gospel music or something. Hope hopped off her bed and went to her closet, where her beautiful white gown hung, wrapped in plastic, off the back of the door.

She was actually getting married. Crazy was about to be a distant memory and normal was where she planned to relocate.

Cheryl McKay (aka The Screenwriter)

Dialogue & Voices Comparison (Sample K)

There are some interesting changes in this scene unrelated to the dialogue, including how Hope feels about her mom, and expansion of the setting description. Feel free to reread this section, keeping those elements in mind. For this chapter, we'll focus on dialogue. While Rene took her time to get into the dialogue of the scene between Hope and her mother, there is a good parallel between what information translated to the script through the dialogue vs. what is shared in the novel. Rene was consistent with the lines and the voice when she could be. The moment the mother prays that Sam and Hope won't leave seems to be far more endearing in the novel than in the script because of the accompanying interior monologue. I also liked the dialogue switch with the three "pleases" that Rene added. It showed CiCi's desperation more than the script did.

I want to call attention to one funny moment Rene added to the novel that involves subtext between Hope and her mother:

> "By the way, if your daddy shows up at the wedding, how about we both take an arm?"
> *No. Not now. Not talk about Daddy.* "Sure, Mom."

See how Hope's inner monologue is the opposite of what the dialogue says? If there is a film version, when her mother makes this suggestion and the actress says "Sure, Mom," we would be able to watch a talented actress react to the situation. We'd see the subtext on her face. The play between text and subtext is one area in a novel you can have such fun, and it can add to the humor or to the heartbreak of the moment if it's a serious scene.

Dialogue Exercise

The following short dialogue exchange is from Cheryl's

script, *Love's a Stage*. It's a romantic comedy where Aly, a 24-year old Marriage and Family Therapist grad student, has always been a collector of vows she hopes to one day make to her future husband. Yet her faith in such vows is rocked by her parents' announcement that they want to end their 30-year marriage. Aly is not about to let this happen without a fight. While she refuses to date Nick (a handsome thespian who has proposed to her at least three semesters in a row), she has a proposal for him. She wants to pretend they are engaged as part of a plot to get her parents to stay together.

The following short dialogue exchange is from the moment in the script where they've just come back from visiting her parents, deep into their charade. Aly expresses her hope that this ploy will work, that her fake wedding day will morph into a vow renewal ceremony between her parents. She's worried this may not work. So while this exchange is about her parents, by the end, subtextually, Nick is talking about himself in relationship to Aly. While that is not stated in the dialogue, if the film were made, viewers should know what he means. I added the "beat" to the dialogue in hopes the actor and director will get my point — that the line is important and is not fully connected to what Nick just said. If I'd put the line continuous from the previous one, I was afraid the subtext would get missed. It would feel like it belonged with the prior thought. It was my way of trying to call attention to it without being so blatant in adding to Nick's line of dialogue, "I should know."

As an exercise in dialogue vs. subtext, take the following exchange of dialogue, and put it in Nick's point of view. Write what he says out loud vs. what he thinks in his mind. Remember: it's supposed to sound like he's talking about her parents — in context of their conversation — yet he's talking about himself and how he feels about her. How he can't make her love him. While they attend Boston University, he's a southern import from the Carolinas. He still has an accent, if you'd like to play with an accent or southern colloquialisms as part of his inner voice. Like Rene often does, feel free to add to the front end and / or the back end of the scene with your own dialogue so the scene is long enough.

```
                    ALY
          You are the best friend I could
          have asked for. I don't know
          what I'm gonna do if this
          doesn't work.

                    NICK
          We'll do what we can, Aly. But
          the rest... it's up to your folks.
                    (beat)
          You can't make someone love you.
```

* * *

I encourage you to do the same exercise with your characters, practicing to write dialogue that is the opposite of thoughts that go on internally.

Next up, in our final chapter, we'll share with you about partnerships between novelists and screenwriters.

Chapter Ten
PARTNERSHIPS

Cheryl McKay (aka The Screenwriter)

When Screenwriters Should Partner with Novelists

After Rene wrote *The Ultimate Gift* film novelization, I knew I wanted to work with her. She had such amazing instincts and insights into my writing. Like I mentioned earlier, I knew when she added a scene from an early script draft she'd never read that she was on my wavelength. I also recognized how opposite the writing rules were between scripts and novels. I needed her expertise if we could sell my scripts as novels. Watching her work on my stories has been an education for me in just how different these writing forms are. It's what inspired us to write this book.

So, when is it a good idea to partner with a novelist and when should a screenwriter consider writing it herself?

Partnering with Rene was the best choice I could have made. She was already an established novelist with a substantial readership and had contacts with publishing houses. I did not have that on my own. If I had tried to sell my stories to those same publishing houses, they would not have sold (especially with me not being proven as a novelist). It was easier for us to get book contracts through her connections and our agent than me going out on my own.

Additionally, Rene had the training and talent to pull it off. While I had been fully trained as a screenwriter, I had not been as a novelist. *Never the Bride* and *Greetings from the*

Flipside would not have been the books they are without Rene's talent for putting pen to paper (or fingers to keys). You would think it would have been easy for me to write *Never the Bride*; after all, Jessie is based on me, isn't she? For a novel in first person, present tense, shouldn't I be able to write my inner voice? (Well, I did, in my nonfiction book *Finally the Bride,* which indeed sounds a lot like Jessie's voice.) But I have no doubt *Never the Bride* is a far better novel because Rene got inside my head rather than me trying to write it. She could be objective; she could use the talent she already had for Point of View and Interior Monologue and other tools from the novelist's creative box that I hadn't learned enough about yet.

I've learned a lot about them since this partnership began, but in the beginning, I didn't know much about them. So often when she'd give me chapters, my jaw would drop over how much she captured my real interior thoughts. You know, the ones I hadn't shared with her. I lived that journey as a single woman who felt like I had been waiting far too long to get married. It was fascinating to watch her write emotions and thoughts I'd had.

So not only was this partnership formed because Rene had the right contacts to set up projects, it was the best choice for the material. I have to admit these books are better because I didn't write my own adaptations. Now that I've learned more about novel writing, I'm more interested in adapting my own scripts that are outside our romantic comedy branding. But I also know the books I write with her have the potential to be much better.

So, as a screenwriter, you need to ask yourself some questions. Do you have the talent to pull off your own adaptation? Do you have an understanding for this particular writing craft to do it yourself? If you don't feel confident you can pull it off, do you have relationships with novelists you feel would be just as passionate about your stories? Are they willing to pitch those to try to get book contracts? A novelist is going to get half the usual advance money on a novelization because she is splitting that money with the screenwriter. So you are going to want to find a partner who is willing to take less and who is interested in writing a story she didn't generate.

As a screenwriter, I often get hired to write book adaptations. Just because the scripts were based on someone else's material doesn't mean I wasn't interested in the job. In the same way, a novelist may also enjoy adapting someone else's work and taking a break from having to create everything from scratch. Do you know that novelist? Is she published? Is she booking contracts regularly? Do you feel you could work with her amicably throughout the process, let her do her craft without micromanaging her creative choices?

If you feel it's not in your best interests to do your adaptations, I encourage you to find the right novelist who is willing to read a script or two of yours, and consider a partnership. As Rene has often said, writing a novelization is half the work. It should be, if the script is in tip-top shape before the novelist takes the job. You need to have done your work as the screenwriter for this to happen. A novelist should not have to do the heavy lifting on structure, plot, and character development. You should give her a great road map to follow.

If you do form a partnership, make sure it's with a novelist you enjoy reading and one who fits your style. This is a relationship you could be in for a long while.

You also need to decide that you will respect her decisions if she writes something in a way you're not sure of or that wouldn't be your preference. She is the novelist and gets the final say. If you trust the person you are working with, you won't mind letting her be the expert she is and letting her have that final say if there is a disagreement between you.

Screenwriters Doing Their Own Novelizations

What if you can't find a novelist as a partner? Should you consider writing your own adaptations? Some of you may prefer that. If you are willing to put the time into learning the craft, studying the form, yes. It will be much harder to sell if you aren't established as a novelist. Yet, self-publishing (or what's often called independent publishing) is an option. I equate it to producing a film independently. If the book does well, that may help you set up a film.

You can decide if you'd like to go for a full-length novel, like I did with *Song of Springhill*, or novella length like I chose for *The Walk* (*Flip Flop Fiction* series).

The story behind the true-life disasters of Springhill was big enough that it deserved some breathing room. But don't feel the pressure if you don't feel like your script would be best as a 80,000-word novel. Novellas and shorter novels are gaining popularity, especially in ebooks. I chose the novella length for *The Walk* because they are based on hour-long television script episodes, not full-length feature film scripts.

If you decide to write your own novel, research proper formatting and study published novels. Follow all the conventions of professionally published novels. I'd suggest finding a template or setting the margins in your document for the correct-sized book in paperback so you can write your draft into the actual book size and format you want to use for publishing. Choose a size conventional for novels of the length you expect it to be. Typing into a document that is sized correctly will help you gauge appropriate chapter lengths and chapter breaks. I also suggest you format the front of your book the way professional books are made, with the usual front matter, including copyright information. Some online sites may suggest as an independent author to just throw it at the back of the book. But this isn't done in the professional world. So, why do it on your independently published novel?

If you do have a chance to work with an established novelist, especially when you're starting out, I strongly suggest it. Being a screenwriter, even with a successful, award-winning movie out there, would not have helped me set up any of my projects at publishing houses. Only partnering with Rene did that. The publishing world is different from the film world; they "get" novelists, not screenwriters. We were halfway through the process on one of our projects before the publisher even remembered I existed. They don't necessarily understand who does what legwork on the project. They don't even read the script itself when we're working on selling our ideas. The script doesn't sell the project; the proposal does.

Novelization Proposals

When as a team we try to sell a script as a novel, what is the sales tool? The script? Not usually. Most publishers would have no idea what to do with a script or how to read one with an eye toward it being adaptable. It's a blueprint for a film; it wouldn't feel weighty enough to them.

We develop proposals for a project instead. I take on most of the work on the proposal part while Rene writes the sample chapter(s). I write sections like:

- Hook (a.k.a logline)
- Genre
- Target Word Count
- Audience
- Story Synopsis (5-10 pages)
- Marketing Information
- Author Bios
- Past Reviews
- Sales Information
- Film Rights Information

Most of the proposals I've written have been at least 15 pages long. The proposal contains a long synopsis, usually about 5-10 pages based on the story from the screenplay. The publishers never see my screenplays. Instead, they see the synopsis with full details about the beginning, middle, and end of the story. Yes, they must know where the story is going. You have to include the twists and turns, and provide the resolution.

Meanwhile, Rene writes a sample chapter or two or

three, depending on the project. If she chooses one point of view for the book, like Jessie in *Never the Bride*, she writes one chapter. If she chooses more than one point of view, like *Greetings from the Flipside*, she writes one chapter for each point of view. *Greetings from the Flipside* had three points of view. The first was in Hope's mind, past tense, third-person, the second was Jake's third-person, past tense point of view, and then for some special sequences called "Greetings from my Life," Hope's voice was in first-person, present tense. Rene felt like it would be best to demonstrate this voice by showing the potential publishers all three points of view in our sample chapters.

Contracts: Who has Rights to What?

So, you are probably wondering who has rights to what material, and what goes in the film rights information in the proposal.

I apologize in advance if this segment makes your head spin a little. We writers like to stick to the creative and not deal with the legal, right? But, trust me, you must understand this area, or you could miss out!

I am a union screenwriter (WGA). There is a term called "separation of rights" where the Writer's Guild protects screenwriters of original screenplays. This protection goes away for any movie based on a book. Separation of rights is a valuable commodity to a screenwriter when applicable. Let me try to help you understand what it is, so you know what you will want to protect specifically as the screenwriter.

If you write an original screenplay, you have separation of rights. You started this story. You have rights related to sequels, spin-offs, remakes, and characters. *Never the Bride* was my original screenplay, so separated rights applies. This is good because I already had a sequel, *Forever the One*, planned before we started our novel partnership. I also can see the project eventually being a television series, with the ongoing gimmick of the show being Jessie's proposals business and having different customers each week. I need the rights to explore these creative options. As the original screenwriter, I have them. This even includes the characters. If someone wanted to make a film or series based on a side character of *Never the Bride*, he'd have to negotiate and pay me for that right. To help you understand that part a little better, let me put it in context of a television show. If you wrote an episode of a crime drama and created a new character—like the family member of victim—let's hope she becomes a love interest for the lead investigator. If so, you would get paid a character payment for every episode that character appears in the future.

However, what about a project like *The Ultimate Gift* that was based on the book by Jim Stovall? Separated rights no longer applies. It's categorized as non-original screenplay—which hopefully is not a commentary on the writing. It gets that label because the screenplay is based on underlying material. When I did the screen adaptation of that film, I created characters like Alexia (the love story character) and Jay (Jason's father). They did not exist in the original book. Jason was Red's grandnephew in the novel, so the author had no reason to include a story about Red's son Jay. I developed backstory for the film about Jason's father and how he died. So, then what happens when the author decides to write a sequel book (*The Ultimate Life*)? He can incorporate characters I created in the first film, like Alexia and Jay, and not compensate or credit me for them. Even though I created them, separated rights do not apply since book one existed first. A movie company would have been free to incorporate them into a sequel film without paying me for it, even if I hadn't been hired to do some writing on it. Yes, at times, that can seem unfair, but it's how it works.

So you see why separated rights on my original screenplays are important for me to preserve, even if I'm selling the rights for them to be novelized?

When Rene and I began our partnership, I needed to protect those rights. I didn't want the film version of any of my novelizations to ever get contracted as if they were based on books, or I would lose creative rights. We had a contract between us that gave her the right to use the material in a book. I retained my "original screenplay" status, even though a movie would be made after the book's release. The chain of what was written and in what order established this too, so it was clear the script came first. I also have an agreement with Rene that anything we come up with in book form can be freely added back into the script, if desired. It gives me 100% rights to that material. This is extremely important because when I sell a script, I have to sign chain of title paperwork for funding to come through. If I don't have rights to the book material as well, it could seriously inhibit my ability to sell scripts.

So, in our novelization proposals that get sent to publishers, we have a clause in there that states 100% of the performance rights will remain with the authors. My separate agreement with Rene shows that 100% goes directly to me and is not shared. While it may be unusual for a publisher to want to grant this at 100%, we had to make it non-negotiable. If the publishers retained any of those, they could option book rights out to a producer or production company. That entity could bypass me as the screenwriter, never look at my script, and hire another writer to do a script based on the novel version. Suddenly, all of my rights to the material would be gone. It would get categorized as a movie based on a book, not my script. So I had to also protect those rights.

Being a union writer, I have rules I must follow. I can't just sell my story to any company that isn't a signatory to the Writer's Guild. So technically, the publishers can't negotiate to sell my stories without me having a part of it. If they could have legally, I would have lost all that work done on scripts, too, if they could bypass me in the process.

So word to the wise: keep your performance rights and keep the right to use what's in the novels. Keep the status as "original screenplay" in any contract you sign, after the book comes out, with a production company. Spell it out.

If you decided to independently publish your script as a novel, you can put a notice on the copyright page that states the novel is based on a screenplay. That way if a producer spots the novel and checks the copyright page for rights and contact information, it will lead that producer back to you, the original screenwriter.

Our publishers retain the rights to do sequel novels, but we have in our contracts we must be the authors to do the work. I didn't want, for example, a sequel novel to get done by a publisher on *Never the Bride* while I had my own sequel script, *Forever the One*, in the works.

One other word about rights with publishers: If you plan to pen books about writing techniques where you want to quote your own work as samples—like we have done with our projects here—try to negotiate into your contracts up front retaining the right to quote a reasonable portion of your work without asking for written permission or paying fees. We did not do this in advance. It creates a lot of legwork on your part to get these permissions later. Sometimes the fees are too cost prohibitive. This is why we were unable to specifically quote novel passages from *Never the Bride* in this book. Lesson learned.

Lastly, if the work the novelist does on the book *significantly* changes your story, structure, and characters—and those changes get implemented into the script—you should consider how to compensate your novelist if a film gets made. Regardless, they will get great rewards when the book rereleases to coincide with the film, and will probably sell a lot more copies than before it was made into a film. So, novelists see great benefits as well, even though their names will not be on the feature films as screenwriters. (The WGA has very strict rules and governs screen credits.)

Here's the disclaimer: Rene and I are not lawyers, so we strongly encourage you to consult one about how to best draft your contracts. This includes the contracts between the authors, with the publisher, and then down the road when you sell your screenplay that has a book in the works or already published.

Okay, your head can stop spinning now as we move onto the next topic.

Working Relationships Between
Novelists & Screenwriters

My first suggestion for novelists: use your screenwriter! Don't be afraid of him. Understand he knows his story better than you ever will from the few reads you give the script before you start your novelization job. He will have read "his masterpiece" probably more than twenty times. He will be able to help guide you, along the way, if you're making choices that may affect the book. The reason your job should be easier than writing a new novel on your own is he put a year or two or more into it before you took on the project.

This doesn't mean you have to feed the screenwriter a chapter at a time. That could get annoying. In the beginning of our projects, I usually see the first few chapters before Rene writes the rest of the first draft. (These are the sample chapters for the proposal.) We can make sure we like the point of view and tone chosen for the project. If there are problems, we can address those before the whole book is written. Sometimes I can pinpoint issues early on that would cause Rene challenges later.

For example, in *Greetings from the Flipside*, I caught in our sample chapters that Rene had forgotten to write in one character's pregnancy. Just simply pointing this out allowed her to incorporate the progression of that pregnancy throughout the first draft, rather than having to go back and add it to the entire book.

Once we both feel we're on a good track, I wait until the first draft is finished to read the rest. Screenwriters, think of it this way. When you write a script, you don't like when a client wants to see pages before the draft is done, right? This is especially true if you are one of those writers, like me, who writes messy first drafts then goes back and rewrites. If I had to keep rewriting my opening pages to make them "client-ready," it may derail my momentum for the rest of the script. Respect your novelist enough to not ask to see pages as you go (unless this is a preference of the novelist). It's best to not interrupt her creative process.

After the first draft is finished, the screenwriter is an excellent resource in continuity. Again, he knows his story better than anyone and is more likely to spot inconsistencies. Don't be threatened by this; use it to your advantage. He can also offer a great set of fresh eyes to find fixes that should happen before it goes to the editor.

This is a partnership that should enhance the writing overall. As a novelist, you are in this because you hopefully like the story enough to want to spend a few months with the characters and the story the screenwriter originally created.

I have to say working with Rene has made me a better writer. So many times she wrote "me" (as Jessie) better than I could have written me. It was humbling and exciting to watch. Sometimes she comes up with wonderful gems in our collaborations that I gladly move over to my screenplays. Other times what she writes is better, yet it doesn't fit the screenplay format. So I just enjoy it in book form.

Whose Name Goes Where

The final subject I'll explore is how to credit the writers on the book. Naturally, since it's a joint effort, both names should go on the book. Some novelizations have the author name and then "based on the screenplay by" with the screenwriter's name. (That usually happens when the novelization is written after the film.) Rene and I have chosen to do this as a co-writing credit, having one name below the other. Our preference is for Rene's name to go first, since this is the book version. We didn't have that on *Never the Bride* for typesetting reasons, but learned an interesting lesson. Rene is the author whose name is known by readers, not my name as the screenwriter. (I mean, really, who knows who most screenwriters are anyway, right?) Because my name went first—purely as a typesetting choice—it meant the book got filed on bookshelves under McKay instead of Gutteridge. So, guess what? Her faithful readers couldn't find it. Not a good idea. So, especially if you are teamed up with an established novelist with a fan base, it's best to go with her name first. Plus, though you've pulled your half of the workload in writing the script by yourself, your novelist has done the lion's share on the novel herself. She doesn't get credit on the screenplay version. So, let this be the moment to have her name above yours.

Rene Gutteridge (aka The Novelist)

Partnerships from the Novelist POV

In my novelization writing career so far, I've worked with scripts in all levels of production. *The Ultimate Gift* was far into post-production by the time I was hired to write the novelization. In fact, I only had a few weeks to get it done, but I also had the advantage of being able to see the movie before I wrote the book.

I've worked with a script that had just finished shooting, one that was beginning to shoot and a few that were not greenlit at all. There were advantages in each of these stages, but one thing they all had in common was the screenwriters were seasoned and working in the industry.

The reason this is important is because first, you want a writer who has some experience working on projects with a team of people. When you have a writer who has no experience with collaboration, you tend to get people who are inflexible and unwilling to allow the necessary changes needed for a good adaptation. Novelists are notorious for this when their books get made into movies. I once read there is a major studio that won't even let novelists step onto the lot. Why? Because novelists don't understand the adaptation process. When their stories must be changed or rearranged or told in different ways, as films must do, their feathers get ruffled. Because they don't understand the process, they become difficult to work with.

I have found, for the most part, that screenwriters are easy to work with. As I said before, they're used to their works being adapted and interpreted. That being said, the more experience a screenwriter has the easier your partnership will be. Like Cheryl has done so beautifully for me time and time again, an experienced screenwriter will deliver to you a solid, well-written script, which will make your job a lot easier. Trying to fill in story holes as you go can make the process longer and more tedious, so make sure you are happy with the script that you're working with before you take the job.

An experienced screenwriter will also have more of a chance of getting her movie made, which is helpful in many ways. Part of the vision for writing a novelization off an unproduced script is the book has a chance for a second life. It is first and foremost released as a novel, to stand on its own, unattached to any production or project. It is, simply, a novel. But if the script goes into production, that's a bonus! The book then can be rereleased with the movie poster on the cover and find itself a second life. Everybody, including the publishing company, the novelist, the screenwriter and the production company, wins. Many novelizations stay as novels only, but having the prospect of that second life is always fun.

One rule to remember—never take a script project assuming it will be made into a movie. There are no guarantees. Even if the movie is in production, shooting as you write, there are no guarantees it will get released. Sometimes securing a distributor can take months, if not years. So every novelization that is written before a final movie is in distribution should be able to stand on its own, without any help from the movie. If a novelization is contracted to release with the movie, the publisher and writer should be prepared for major delays because of the unpredictability of the moviemaking process.

Another helpful tip is to sit down with the screenwriter and explain the process of the partnership. The screenwriter should understand this is not co-writing, but rather adaptation. Clearly spell out the involvement you expect the screenwriter to have and the room you will need to write the book. The more communication there is up front, the happier both parties will be in the end. When you meet with the screenwriter, try to get a sense of how well she communicates. One of the things that has made my partnership with Cheryl so viable and productive and successful is that we have a great working relationship. Cheryl trusts me. When she has a question about why I've written something a certain way, she allows me to explain. When I first told Cheryl I thought *Never the Bride* should be written in first-person present tense, I could hear the alarm in her voice. But she allowed me to talk through the reasoning behind it—why I felt the story would benefit from the immediate scene that present tense allows for. She was still hesitant before we began, but after I showed her a few chapters, she was on board.

In my partnership with John Ward for *Heart of the Country*, we were having a conference call where I was spelling out my very unusual vision for this story. This was where I explained my desire to use multiple first-person, which I mentioned before is a very rarely used technique where you write in first person with every character. I felt such a connection to each of the characters in John's story I felt I wanted to go really deep with each of them. John jokes that he was Googling this even as we talked because he had no idea what I was talking about. But in the end, John trusted me to do what I felt was best for the novel.

Because *Heart of the Country* was in pre-production when we partnered with John, John was kind enough to allow the publishing house and me a glimpse into the casting process. It was always so exciting to get an email from John when he'd made a decision about who he'd cast in what role. Because I was now so immersed in these characters, it was a treat to see into this side of the filmmaking.

Typically the novelist and screenwriter split all

advances and royalties. It's the fairest way to compensate. The novelist is doing half the work of a regular novel. Working from a screenplay is like working from a detailed outline. The screenwriter is paid for the material he's providing to the novelist. The novelist should also be prepared to understand that some original material from the book may land in the movie, without writer credit. It might be tempting to ask for some credit for this, but that would begin a complicated process that isn't worth your time and effort. When some of my writing has ended up in a movie, I am satisfied just knowing the screenwriter liked it so much he put it in there. As Cheryl discussed about the rights, the screenwriter owns the entire creative property of the project as it has to do with the film. So walk away knowing you've done a good job and that you've captured the vision of the screenwriter so well that he wants to find a way to fit in the material.

Through writing novelizations, I've learned to love the collaborative process. Novel writing can be a lonely business, but partnering with another creative writer can be immensely satisfying. It has taught me a lot about being gracious and giving within the creative process. The honor of another writer allowing me to adapt his or her baby has become a precious and heartwarming thing for me.

I learn a lot from the screenwriters I work with, in writing and in life in general. To me, they are such brave souls. When they write a script, they know so much will be changed or left on the cutting room floor. To watch them let go of control of their vision has inspired me to listen more carefully to others who are involved in my projects, taking into account all ideas and looking for places to implement them.

Recently I heard from Rik Swartzwelder, the screenwriter and director for *Old Fashioned*, of which I partnered for the novelization. Rik had just finished editing the film down, which meant he had some difficult choices to make about what was kept and what was left on the cutting room floor. He said he was so thankful to have the novelization because he now has a version of the story that has all the scenes and dialogue he wanted to keep. That really warmed my heart. It had become more than a project to him. It had become a treasure. And as a novelist, there is nothing more gratifying to hear.

I am so proud of the work Cheryl and I have accomplished, as well as what I've done with other screenwriters. The merging of these two worlds—the novelization—has forged a new frontier in the world of writing, and we're happy to be a part of it. So screenwriters, novelists: take the tips you've learned in this book and go make some dreams come true!

The Authors Wish to
Gratefully Acknowledge:

B&H Publishing
Janet Kobobel Grant
Denise McKay
Christopher Price
Susan Rohrer
Rik Swartzwelder
Tyndale House Publishers
John Ward
Waterbrook Press / Random House
Our Heavenly Father

About the Authors

Rene Gutteridge is the award-winning and best-selling author of twenty-one novels, including her latest releases *Misery Loves Company* (suspense), *Greetings from the Flipside* (comedy) and *Heart of the Country* (drama). Her recent suspense titles also include *Listen, Possession* and *Escapement.* She has novelized six screenplays and movies, including two new releases due out in 2014, *Just 18 Summers* and *Old Fashioned.* Her romantic comedy with screenwriter Cheryl McKay, *Never the Bride,* won the Carol Award in 2010 for Best Women's Fiction. Her indie film, the comedy *SKID,* which is based on her novel, is in post-production and due to release in 2014. She is also a creative consultant on *Boo,* a film based on her beloved novel series, which is in development at Sodium Entertainment with Andrea Nasfell (*Mom's Night Out*) as the screenwriter. She is also co-writer in a collaborative comedy project called *Last Resort* with screenwriters Torry Martin and Marshal Younger. Find her on Facebook and Twitter or at her website, **www.renegutteridge.com**.

* * *

Cheryl McKay has been professionally writing since 1997. Tommy Nelson served as her first publisher, teaming her with Frank Peretti on the *Wild and Wacky, Totally True Bible Stories* series. Cheryl wrote the screenplay adaptation of *The Ultimate Gift*, the feature film starring Academy Award Nominees James Garner and Abigail Breslin. It's based on Jim Stovall's best-selling novel. The film was released by Fox in  theaters in Spring 2007 and has won such awards as the Crystal Heart Award, the Crystal Dove, one of the Top Ten Family Movies at MovieGuide Awards, and a CAMIE Award. She also wrote the DVD for *Gigi: God's Little Princess*, another book adaptation based on the book by Sheila Walsh. She wrote a half-hour drama for teenagers about high school violence, called *Taylor's Wall*, produced in Los Angeles by Family Theater Productions. After winning a fellowship, she was commissioned to write a feature script, *Greetings from the Flipside*, for Art Within, which Gutteridge and McKay released as a novel through B&H Publishing in October 2013. Her screenplay, *Never the Bride*, was adapted into a novel by Gutteridge and was released by Waterbrook Press in June 2009. The film version is in development. As one passionate for those who are losing hope in their wait to find love, she released the non-fiction version, *Finally the Bride: Finding Hope While Waiting*. She also penned her autobiography, *Finally Fearless: Journey from Panic to Peace*. She wrote the screen story for *The Ultimate Life*, the sequel to *The Ultimate Gift*. Find her on Facebook, Twitter, Pinterest, or at her website, **www.purplepenworks.com** or **www.finallyone.com**.

Check out the full-length novelizations of the samples used
in this book, on sale now at book retailers:

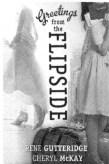

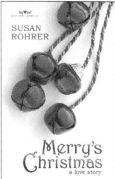

Coming Soon:
Old Fashioned (Rene Gutteridge & Rik Swartzwelder)

Just 18 Summers (Rene Gutteridge with Michelle Cox, Marshal
Younger & Torry Martin)

Song of Springhill: a love story (Cheryl McKay)

41225986R00104

Made in the USA
Lexington, KY
04 May 2015